# Logo Design 4

LOONEY TUNES

# LogoDesign4

*The International Collection of Logo Design*
*Logogestaltung im internationalen Überblick*
*Une compilation internationale sur le design de logos*

Publisher and Creative Director: B. Martin Pedersen

Editor: Heinke Jenssen
Assistant Editors: April Heck, Vivian Babuts, Laura Cramer

Art Director: Massimo Acanfora
Graphic Designers: Delfin Chavez, Carol Ford
Photographer: Alfredo Parraga

Published by Graphis Inc.

*(opposite)* Design Firm: Landor Associates Client: Warner Bros.

# Contents Inhalt Sommaire




*Remarks:* We extend our heartfelt thanks to contributors throughout the world who have made it possible to publish a wide and international spectrum of the best work in this field. Entry instructions for all Graphis Books may be requested from: **Graphis Inc.**, 141 Lexington Avenue, New York, NY 10016-8193 or visit our Web site, www.graphis.com

*Anmerkungen*: Unser Dank gilt den Einsendern aus aller Welt, die es uns durch ihre Beiträge ermøglicht haben, ein breites, internationales Specktrum der besten Arbeiten zu veröffentlichen. Teilnahmebedingungen für die Graphis-Bücher sind erhältlich bei: **Graphis Inc.**, 141 Lexington Avenue, New York, NY 10016-8193. Besuchen Sie uns im World Wide Web, www.graphis.com

*Remerciements:* Toute notre reconnaissance va aux designers du monde entier dont les envois nous ont permis de constituer un vaste panorama international des meilleures création. Les modalités d'inscription peuvent être obtenues auprès de: **Graphis Inc.**, 141 Lexington Avenue, New York, NY 10016-8193. Rendez-nous visite sur notre site web: www.graphis.com

ISBN: 1-888001-58-5


Printed by Doosan Dong-A Co., Ltd..

*(opposite)* Design Firm: Sandstrom Design Client: Pavlov Productions *(next page)* Design Firm: Mires Design Client: Hell Racer

HELLRACER

Commentary Kommentar Commentaire

## Three Logos

*There aren't enough pages within this book to present our readers with all of the outstanding logo designs that Graphis received. However, we did take some time to illuminate a few that, for whatever, intangible reasons, were especially eye-catching. Happily, these also represent the work of design firms from different places in the world, providing a global vantage point of what's happening now with logo design. Our gratitude extends to the respective designers and clients who took time to reflect on both the business and creative aspects of their respective logo designs, and who offered a glimpse into their particular success stories.*

**Studio Bortolotti: Saralva Logo** This fluid, appealing new logo for Saralva was designed by Italy's Studio Bortolotti—who were hired, comments Saralva's director Gianfranco Saralvo, because of their reputation of "long-standing professionalism and well-known talent." The commission proved a smart move for the company, a leading national manufacturer of women's stockings and tights. "Our market research demonstrates that the new logo has been well received by our customers," Saralvo continues, "and has given power to the corporate identity of our firm. It distinguishes us from our competitors, and we have seen a vast development in our notoriety. Our investment in a new logo has paid off with remarkable success."

On first look, the observer will instantly recognize the letter "S," a subtle "C" or two, and perhaps a hint of the yin and yang sign. Certainly, the clean design contains a sense of motion as well as a satisfying symmetry (it reads the same upside-down). The real thinking behind the design? Gianni Bortolotti explains: "The logo is the interpretation of the characters "c" for calze (stockings or tights) and "S" for Saralva. Its form was inspired by flexibility, especially associated with the curves of the female body. Throughout the creative process, we kept in mind the pragmatic, syntactic, and semantic aspects that are typical of symbolic language." Bortolotti once said that we need to "contemporize the 'less is more' of Mies." As evidenced by this logo—really just three strokes of the pen, brilliantly arranged—he is a man who likes to practice what he preaches.

**Graphics and Designing Inc: G & D Logo** The creation of this futuristic logo—something like M.C. Escher meets the space age—was designed by Mr. Hayashi of Tokyo's Graphics and Designing Inc., who passionately describes the creative process as somewhat similar to childbearing. "At our office," he says, "you hear the first cries of joy and occasionally, the painful groans."

He explains their company's philosophy that commercial design is a type of alchemy. Drawing upon the colorful metaphor of an egg, Hayashi says: "The purpose of design or works of art is to yield financial success, but even more important, the true intention of design and art is to raise the quality of living for client and consumer alike. We designers must not be satisfied with merely depicting an ordinary white egg as an extraordinary one. We must present the egg to be as special as a golden egg."

Recalling the logo's creation process, Hayashi comments, "My quest was to capture the essence of existence, in light of the famous prayer by Han-nya-shin-kyo, 'All that exists, exists in vain.'" The fanciful, architectural details are, he says, embodiments of structures and cities taken from as far back as medieval Europe and the London of Jules Verne, as well as present day, ever-modern Tokyo.

**Joseph Rattan Design: Grammarian Group Logo** The efficiency of this logo is hard to deny—the double "G," of course, takes its source from the client's name, while also visually reinforcing its alliteration. Furthermore, says, Joseph Rattan, the New York design firm's creative director, "a type solution seemed natural for a writer's association." (The Grammarian Group is an organization that provides an informal forum for freelance writers and editors to share insights on a variety of topics.) Rattan continues, reflecting on his firm's creative approach, "We came up with strong intellectual content, then eliminated unnecessary elements that would destroy the content or design. This clean rendering style produces a mark that will age well and is less likely, than more heavily styled marks, to become dated."

Mary Langridge, the director of the Grammarian Group, was delighted with the results. "We wanted a logo that was clean, memorable, and above all, not 'wordy'—and that's exactly what Joe gave us." Even more, she explains, the introduction of the logo encouraged group members and public alike to take them more seriously. "It [the logo] gave us credibility, and we began to see ourselves as a professional association, not just an ad hoc gripe group," she says. "What fun it is having Joe come back to us with a logo of this caliber. For once, we were speechless."

# Drei Logo-Designs

*Leider reicht der zur Verfügung stehende Platz in diesem Buch nicht aus, um auf alle hervorragenden Logos einzugehen, die Graphis erhalten hat. Wir haben deshalb stellvertretend einige ausgewählt, die, aus welchen Gründen auch immer, besonders auffällig sind und aus verschiedenen Ländern kommen, in der Hoffnung, dadurch wenigstens ein Gefühl von dem zu vermitteln, was international in diesem Bereich passiert. Wir danken den betroffenen Designern und ihren Auftraggebern, dass sie sich die Zeit genommen haben, über die geschäftlichen und kreativen Aspekte ihrer Logos nachzudenken und damit einen Einblick in diese Erfolgsgeschichten zu ermöglichen.*

**Studio Bortolotti: Saralva-Logo.** Das neue Logo für Saralva, das durch seine geschmeidige Form besticht, wurde vom Studio Bortolotti, Italien, entworfen. Gemäss Gianfranco Saralva, Direktor dieses Herstellers von Strumpfwaren für Damen, wurde Bortolotti aufgrund seines langjährigen guten Rufes als professionelles und kreatives Design-Studio engagiert. Das erwies sich als eine ausgesprochen kluge Wahl: «Unsere Marktforschung hat ergeben, dass das neue Logo bei unseren Kundinnen gut angekommen ist», sagt Saralvo weiter, «und dass es dem Erscheinungsbild der Firma gut getan hat. Es verhilft uns gegenüber der Konkurrenz zu einem unverwechselbaren Auftritt, und wir haben festgestellt, dass sich der Bekanntheitsgrad unserer Firma wesentlich gesteigert hat. Unsere Investition in ein neues Logo hat sich dank des Erfolgs eindeutig bezahlt gemacht».

Auf den ersten Blick erkennt man den Buchstaben ‚S', ein subtiles ‚C' oder auch zwei und vielleicht noch eine Andeutung des Zeichens für Yin und Yang. Eindeutig vermittelt das klare Design ein Gefühl von Bewegung sowie eine angenehme Ausgewogenheit (es bleibt unverändert, wenn man es auf den Kopf stellt). Die tatsächlichen Überlegungen, die hinter dem Design stehen? Gianni Bortolotti erklärt: «Das Logo ist eine Interpretation der Buchstaben C für Calze (Strümpfe und Strumpfhosen) und S für Saralva. Die mit weiblichen Formen assoziierte Geschmeidigkeit lieferte die Grundidee für die Form des Logos. Während des gesamten kreativen Prozesses hatten wir die für die symbolische Sprache typischen pragmatischen, syntaktischen und semantischen Aspekte im Kopf.» Bortolotti erwähnt weiter, dass man Mies van der Rohes Credo «Weniger ist mehr» unserer Zeit anpassen muss. Wie man an diesem Logo erkennen kann – eigentlich nur drei brillant arrangierte Striche – ist er ein Mann, der befolgt, was er predigt.

**Graphics and Designing Inc.: G & D Logo.** Dieses futuristische Logo – in der Art ‚M.C. Escher trifft auf das Raumzeitalter' – wurde von Mr. Hayashi von Graphics and Designing Inc. in Tokio entworfen. Mit grosser Leidenschaft beschreibt er den kreativen Prozess als «etwas, das einer Geburt gleichkommt. In unserem Büro hörte man die ersten Freudenschreie und gelegentlich schmerzerfülltes Stöhnen.»

Hinsichtlich der Firmenphilosophie sagt er, «kommerzielles Design ist eine Art von Alchemie». Er benutzt bei seiner Umschreibung die ausdrucksvolle Metapher eines Eis: «Der Zweck von Design oder Kunstwerken ist die Erzielung eines finanziellen Erfolges, aber noch wichtiger ist, dass die wahre Bestimmung von Design und Kunst die Erhöhung der Lebensqualität sowohl für den Kunden als auch für den Konsumenten ist. Wir Designer dürfen uns nicht damit zufrieden geben, ein gewöhnliches weisses Ei als etwas Besonderes darzustellen. Wir müssen das Ei so darstellen, als sei es ein goldenes Ei.»

In Bezug auf die Entwicklung des speziellen Logos erklärt er: «Ich habe mich bemüht, das Wesentliche des Seins einzufangen, im Lichte des berühmten Gebets von Han-nya-hin-kyo: «Alles, das existiert, existiert umsonst.» Die phantasievollen architektonischen Details seien, wie er sagt, Verkörperungen von Strukturen und Städten aus dem Europa des Mittelalters und dem London von Jules Verne sowie des heutigen, modernen Tokios.

**Joseph Rattan Design: Grammarian Group Logo.** Beim Anblick dieses Logos sagte der Creative Director von Graphis, dass er den Gestalter gern kennenlernen würde. Die Effektivität des Logos ist in der Tat nicht zu leugnen – das doppelte G bezieht sich natürlich auf den Namen des Kunden, wobei der Stabreim visuell verstärkt wird. Ausserdem boten sich gemäss Joseph Rattan, Creative Director der Firma, «die Buchstaben als natürliche Lösung für einen Schriftstellerverband an». (Die Grammarian Group ist eine Organisation, die freien Schriftstellern und Redakteuren ein informelles Forum für den Erfahrungsaustausch in diversen Bereichen bietet.) Was die kreative Auffassung seiner Firma betrifft, so erwähnt Rattan weiter: «Wir entwickelten einen starken intellektuellen Inhalt und eliminierten dann unnötige Elemente, die den Inhalt oder das Design störten.» Die saubere Ausführung führte zu einem Zeichen, das auch nach einiger Zeit noch gut aussehen wird – im Gegensatz zu sehr ‚gestylten' Zeichen, die schnell altmodisch wirken.»

Mary Langridge, Direktorin der Grammarian Group, war über die Ergebnisse hocherfreut. «Wir wollten ein sauberes, unvergessliches Logo, das auf keinen Fall ‚wortreich' sein sollte – und genau das lieferte Joe uns.» Darüber hinaus habe das Logo bewirkt, dass die Mitglieder und auch die Öffentlichkeit den Verband ernster nehmen. «Es (das Logo) gab uns Glaubwürdigkeit, und wir begannen, uns als professionellen Verband zu sehen, nicht einfach als eine zusammengewürfelte Gruppe», sagt sie. «Es war eine Freude, als Joe uns dieses Logo vorlegte. Für einmal waren wir sprachlos.»

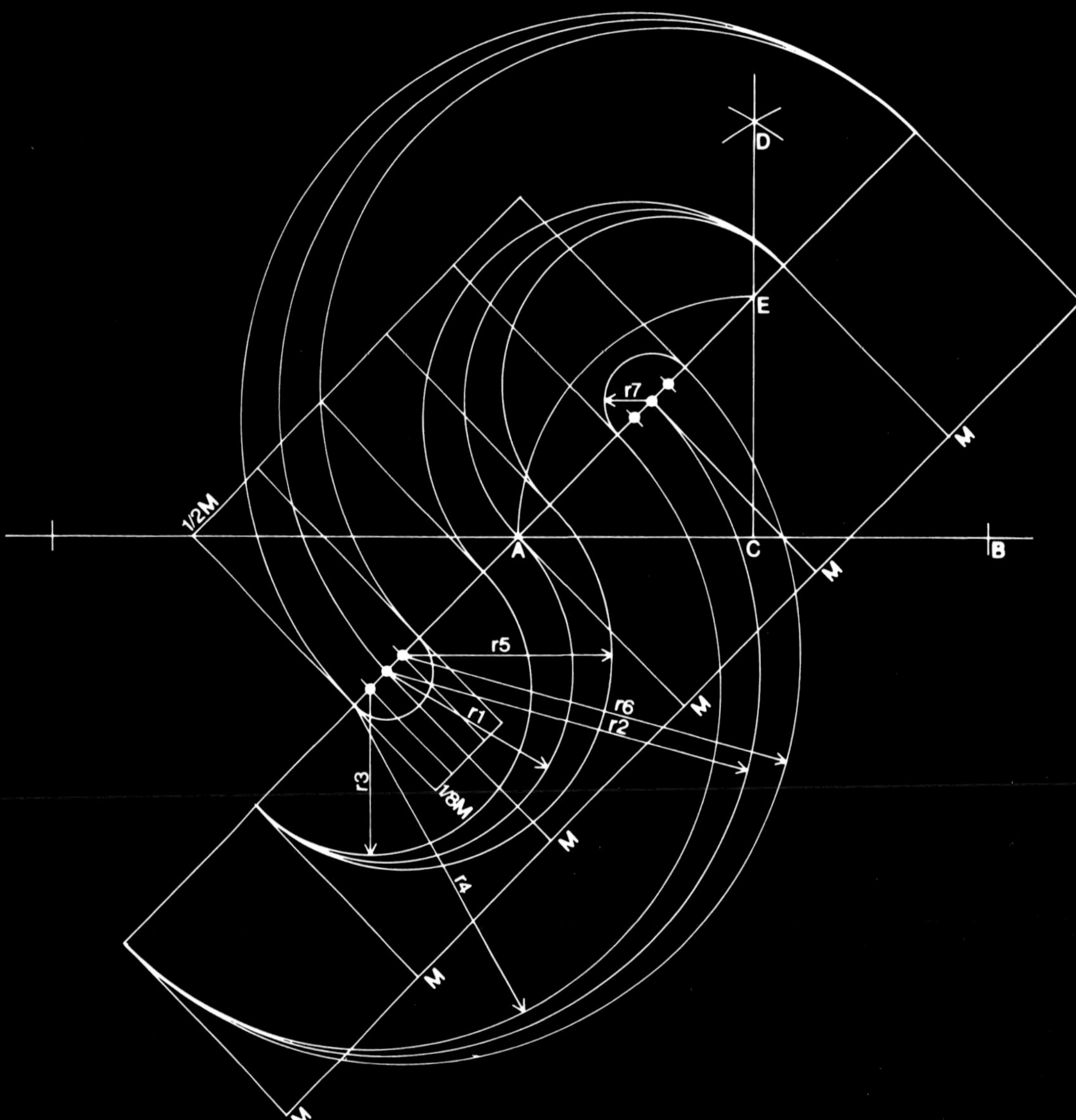

D
E
r7
M
1/2M
A
C
B
M
r5
r6
r2
M
r1
r3
1/8M
M
r4
M
M

## Trois designs de logo

*Malheureusement, nous n'avons pu, faute de place, publier de plus amples commentaires sur les logos présentés par Graphis. Nous avons donc dû faire un choix et avons retenu les logos les plus accrocheurs à nos yeux – pour quelque raison que ce soit –, en espérant que leurs diverses provenances vous donneront un aperçu sur ce qui se passe dans le monde. Nous tenons à remercier tous les designers et commanditaires qui ont bien voulu se pencher sur les aspects commerciaux et créatifs de leurs logos et nous dévoiler les dessous de leur success story.*

**Studio Bortolotti: logo Saralva.** Le studio italien Bortolotti a conçu ce nouveau design aux formes fluides pour le fabricant de bonneterie Saralva. Selon Gianfranco Saralva, directeur de l'entreprise, l'excellente réputation et la longue expérience professionnelle et créative de l'agence Bortolotti ont fait pencher la balance en sa faveur. Un choix qui s'est révélé des plus judicieux: «Notre étude du marché a prouvé que le logo a reçu un accueil favorable de notre clientèle et qu'il a renforcé l'image de notre société. Ce logo nous démarque de nos concurrents, et nous avons constaté qu'il a largement contribué à augmenter notre notoriété. Face au succès rencontré par ce logo, nos investissements se sont avérés plus que payants.»

Au premier coup d'œil, on reconnaît la lettre «S», un «C» subtil ou deux, et probablement une allusion au symbole du Yin et du Yang. Ce design soigné dégage résolument une impression de mouvement et d'équilibre parfait – regardé à l'envers, il est identique. Quelle est la réflexion qui sous-tend ce design? Selon Bortolotti, «le logo est une interprétation de la lettre 'C' pour 'calze' (en italien chaussettes ou bas) et de la lettre 'S' pour Saralva. La douceur associée aux formes féminines nous a livré l'idée de base pour la forme du logo. Durant tout le processus créatif, nous avons gardé à l'esprit tous les aspects pragmatiques, syntaxiques et sémantiques du langage symbolique.» Bortolotti a déclaré un jour que le «moins c'est plus» de Mies van der Rohe devait être adapté à notre époque. Comme ce logo réduit à sa plus simple expression en témoigne – en fait, trois simples traits brillamment arrangés –, Bortolotti est un homme de parole.

**Graphics and Designing Inc.: logo G & D.** Ce logo futuriste – dans le genre M.C. Escher entre dans l'ère interplanétaire – a été conçu par Hayashi de l'agence Graphics and Designing Inc. de Tokyo. C'est avec une grande ferveur qu'il décrit le processus créatif comme «un acte qui ressemble à la naissance d'un enfant. Dans notre bureau, vous entendez les premiers cris de joie et, de temps à autre, des gémissements de douleur.»

Pour parler de la philosophie d'entreprise, une autre métaphore étrange lui vient à l'esprit, celle de l'œuf: «Le design commercial est une sorte d'alchimie. La finalité du design et des œuvres d'art est d'obtenir un succès financier, mais aussi, et c'est bien plus important, d'améliorer la qualité de vie du client et celle du consommateur. Nous autres designers, nous ne devons pas nous contenter de représenter un blanc d'œuf comme quelque chose de spécial. Nous devons représenter l'œuf comme s'il était d'or.»

Questionné sur le développement de son logo, il dit: «Je me suis efforcé de capter l'essence de l'existence à la lumière de la célèbre prière de Han-nya-shin-kyo: 'Tout ce qui existe existe en vain'.» Les détails architectoniques, signes d'une imagination fertile, symbolisent, selon lui, des structures et des villes de l'Europe moyenâgeuse, du Londres de Jules Verne et du Tokyo moderne d'aujourd'hui.

**Joseph Rattan Design: Grammarian Group Logo.** A la vue de ce logo, le directeur créatif de Graphis, vivement impressionné, a déclaré qu'il aimerait bien faire la connaissance de ce concepteur. L'impact de ce logo est en effet indiscutable. La représentation visuelle du double G, qui se réfère naturellement au nom du client, renforce l'allitération. En outre, comme l'explique Joseph Rattan, directeur créatif de la société, «cette solution semblait tout à fait appropriée pour un cercle d'auteurs.» (Le Grammarian Group est une organisation qui offre un forum informel où les écrivains et rédacteurs peuvent échanger leurs idées.) En ce qui concerne l'approche créative de son agence, il déclare: «Nous avons développé un contenu exigeant au niveau intellectuel, puis avons retranché les éléments inutiles qui faisaient de l'ombre au contenu ou au design. Grâce à sa réalisation soignée, ce logo a encore de beaux jours devant lui contrairement à nombre de logos hyperstylisés qui vieillissent très mal.»

Mary Langridge, directrice du Grammarian Group, ne tarit pas d'éloges sur ce logo: «Nous voulions un logo propre et inoubliable, qui ne devait pas être trop 'verbeux'. Et c'est exactement ce que Joe nous a livré.» Grâce à ce logo, l'association a en outre gagné en crédibilité auprès de ses membres et du public en général. «Notre crédibilité s'en est trouvée renforcée et nous avons commencé à nous voir comme une association professionnelle et non plus comme un simple groupe de gens rassemblés au hasard des rencontres. Nous avons ressenti une telle joie lorsque Joe est arrivé avec ce logo. Pour une fois, nous sommes restés sans voix.»

IBM

Microsoft

BOEING

## Logo Means Business: Rick Eiber

**A Nod to the Past: IBM and Westinghouse** Whenever a discussion of corporate identity and business heats up, it's only nanoseconds until the legendary work of the late Paul Rand comes up. What better place to begin, then, than at the beginning: IBM and Westinghouse, the two landmark identity programs launched by Rand. Rand's IBM program in the mid-fifties broke new ground. As part of the original program, he created logo variations which were both diverse and surprising. A striped version was designed as an attention-getting device, one that suggested efficiency and speed, and also managed to tie together three letters whose forms were hard to unify.

He developed both an 8-line and 13-line logo, the latter intended for applications requiring restraint, like legal documents. A specific blue was designated as IBM Blue—a decision that quickly earned the company its moniker "Big Blue" through its consistent, widespread application. Now, fast forward to the nineties: the integrity and quality of the original IBM logo is not merely maintained, but almost revered, by both its owner and astute business people everywhere. Here is a logo known and recognized worldwide, and one that has proven, hands-down, that better design leads to better business.

In 1960, for a fee of $50,000, Rand created the timeless "W" logo for Westinghouse. (Just try to find a deal like that today!) Rand took an existing underlined "W" symbol and modified it, adding distinctive ball-shaped knobs at the ends of the letter's arms—reportedly symbolizing a reactor. Interestingly, the opening of his initial graphics-identification manual states: "Westinghouse has committed itself to a long range design program... Before this design effort can have meaning for our customers, however, the people on all levels of management must see and understand its purpose." Rand seemed to instinctively know: without this kind of understanding, an identity program cannot thrive. In fact, it would be lucky to survive total implementation. The Circle W symbol was the key to Westinghouse's entire graphic design program and remains so today. Other elements of the program included a corporate color, typeface and specially designed logo created with this typeface. Westinghouse's first small investment has paid huge dividends, increasing the value of parent company assets by millions of dollars in intellectual property.

**Logo Design Now: Microsoft and Boeing** When Microsoft first asked me to redraw their logo, they explained part of their dissatisfaction with the existing one: "It isn't legible when reversed out of solid colors or reduced to a small scale"—two crucial qualities if a logo is to be widely applied and read. The six-figure fee and year-long effort included creating a series of publication grids and an extensive new color palette for company-wide use. Microsoft understood the importance of nomenclature as an element of identity. Therefore, they incorporated their public name into each product name—Microsoft Word®, for instance: one logo, one identity, one name. (And one stock, I might add, with which I wish they had paid me, since it has multiplied in value while my greenbacks continue to lose buying power.)

My first work with Boeing was twelve years ago. As an outside consultant specializing in identity and already working with a commercial airplane company, I was asked by Boeing to integrate their newly acquired deHaviland company in Canada. I explained that if each company continued to head off with its own name and look, then it hardly made any difference. And unless Boeing put its own house in order, there would be no program at all. An analysis of the nomenclature and materials led to a straw horse solution to show exactly how, or whether, problems might be resolved. This, in turn, led to the first commission of a corporate identity in the company's 75-year history.

Boeing's merger last year with McDonnell Douglas brought a whole new set of problems. Here were two heavy weights face-to-face, each wanting representation in the new Boeing. Fritz Johnston, McDonnell Douglas' Manager of Corporate Identity, asked if I could update the company's existing symbol. He wanted me to resolve its visual problems, (for one thing, he said, it looked like "a missile being fired at a plane") and still make it compatible with the existing Boeing logotype. In the new symbol, the space element now circles the "globe," and the modified plane form can be read either as a commercial jetliner moving from left to right or a defense "B" wing aircraft coming toward you. These elements reinforced the aerospace orientation of most business segments, while incorporating qualities of both pre-existing identities. The new signature realized the "one company, one vision" attitude requested by Boeing's chairman, Phil Condit. It helped merge two different cultures and reduce conversion/transition expenses. And as we all know, saving money is near and dear to the heart of every business, everywhere.

In today's new global marketplace, mergers and acquisitions lead to new, large, well-financed, visually sophisticated corporate entities continually raising the bar for everyone—but making it tough for small or start-up players to even play the game. Logo design is one of the most effective business tools a CEO can use to level the playing field. A single, bold graphic device can draw immediate recognition for an aspiring player, whether new or old. As the former head of British Rail once said, "Design is intelligence made visible." Indeed, great logo design is a company made visible. And that makes business sense, anytime, anywhere.

***Rick Eiber*** *is an internationally recognized specialist in corporate identity and brand management based near Seattle, Washington. He is the author/editor of* WORLD TRADEMARKS: 100 YEARS *from Graphis Press and a member of Alliance Graphique Internationale (AGI). Rick's works have been honored with hundreds of juried awards and selections for publications worldwide.*

## Ein Logo bedeutet Geschäfte: Rick Eiber

**Ein Blick in die Vergangenheit: IBM und Westinghouse.** Sobald sich die Diskussion über Corporate Identity und Geschäftserfolg aufheizt, dauert es erfahrungsgemäss nur wenige Sekunden, bis die Sprache auf die legendäre Arbeit des verstorbenen Paul Rand kommt. Am besten fängt man am Anfang an, d.h. bei IBM und Westinghouse bzw. den beiden bahnbrechenden C.I.-Programmen, die von Rand lanciert wurden. Mit seinem C.I.-Programm für IBM betrat Paul Rand Neuland. Als Teil des Originalprogramms schuf er zahlreiche, umwerfende Variationen des Logos. Eine gestreifte Variante war als Blickfang gedacht, als Zeichen für Effizienz und Geschwindigkeit. Gleichzeitig entstand dadurch eine Verbindung der drei Buchstaben, deren Form sich eigentlich jeglicher Verschmelzung widersetzte. Er entwarf das Logo mit 8 und mit 13 Streifen, wobei letztere Variante für offizielle Zwecke wie Verträge und andere Dokumente gedacht war. Ein bestimmtes Blau wurde zum IBM-Blau – was der Firma dank der konsequenten und breiten Anwendung den Spitznamen "Big Blue" einbrachte. Macht man einen Sprung in die neunziger Jahre, so stellt man fest, dass Integrität und Charakteristik des Originalentwurfs des IBM-Logos nicht nur beibehalten wurden, sondern mit Ehrfurcht behandelt werden, und zwar von seinem Inhaber wie von allen Geschäftsleuten, die etwas davon verstehen. Hier haben wir ein Logo, das weltweit bekannt und anerkannt ist, eines, das bewiesen hat, dass besseres Design ganz einfach zu besseren Geschäften führt.

Für ein Honorar von $50000 kreierte Rand 1960 das klassische «W»-Logo für Westinghouse. (Heute ist ein solcher Deal kaum mehr denkbar!) Rand nahm das bereits existierende unterstrichene «W»-Symbol und veränderte es, indem er auf die Enden der Aufstriche kleine Kugeln setzte – offenbar als Symbole für einen Reaktor. Interessanterweise steht in der Einführung seines ursprünglichen Design-Manuals: «Westinghouse hat sich einem langfristigen Designprogramm verschrieben.... Bevor dieses Design jedoch für unsere Kunden Bedeutung erlangen kann, müssen die Mitarbeiter aller Management-Stufen seinen Zweck erkennen und verstehen.» Rand schien instinktiv zu wissen, dass ein Identitäts-Design-Programm ohne dieses Verständnis nicht greifen kann. Es wäre andernfalls ein Wunder gewesen, wenn es überhaupt zu einer Einführung in allen Bereichen gekommen wäre.

Das W-Symbol war und ist noch heute der Schlüssel zum gesamten Design-Programm von Westinghouse. Andere Elemente des Programms sind eine Firmenfarbe, eine Schrift und ein speziell entworfener Namenszug in dieser Schrift. Die erste kleine Investition der Firma Westinghouse hat ihr riesige Dividenden eingebracht, indem die Aktivposten der Muttergesellschaft im Bereich des geistigen Eigentums um Millionen von Dollars gesteigert wurden.

**Logo Design heute: Microsoft und Boeing.** Als die Leute von Microsoft mich mit der Überarbeitung ihres Logo beauftragten, erklärten sie zuerst einmal, warum sie mit dem vorhandenen nicht zufrieden waren: «Es ist unlesbar, sobald es negativ auf Grundfarben oder kleiner gedruckt wird» – zwei wichtige Voraussetzungen, wenn ein Logo vielseitig einsetzbar und erkennbar sein soll. Das sechsstellige Honorar und die einjährige Arbeit umfasste eine Reihe von Rastern für die Publikationen und eine umfangreiche neue Farbpalette für den gesamten Geschäftsbereich. Microsoft war sich der Bedeutung einer Nomenklatur als Bestandteil des Erscheinungsbildes bewusst. Die Firma verwendete deshalb ihren Namen bei jedem Produkt – Microsoft Word zum Beispiel: ein Logo, eine Identität, ein Name. (Ich will noch erwähnen, dass ich wünschte, sie hätten mich mit Aktien bezahlt, denn deren Wert hat sich vervielfacht, während meine Dollars immer mehr an Kaufkraft verlieren.)

Meine erste Arbeit für Boeing liegt zwölf Jahre zurück. Als externer Berater, der Spezialist für C.I.-Programme ist und bereits für eine kommerzielle Luftfahrtgesellschaft arbeitete, wurde ich von Boeing beauftragt, die von ihnen neu übernommene kanadische Firma deHaviland zu integrieren. Ich erklärte ihnen, dass kaum etwas bewirkt werden könnte, wenn jede Firma unter ihrem eigenen Namen und Auftritt weitermachen würde. Und wenn Boeing nicht für Ordnung im eigenen Hause sorgen würde, gäbe es kein Programm. Eine Analyse der Nomenklatur und Materialien führte zu einer inoffiziellen Lösung, die genau aufzeigen sollte, wie oder ob Probleme zu lösen wären. Dies wiederum führte zum ersten Auftrag für ein C.I.-Designprogramm in der 75jährigen Geschichte des Unternehmens.

Boeings kürzliche Fusion mit McDonnell Douglas brachte eine ganze Reihe neuer Probleme mit sich. Hier standen sich zwei Schwergewichte gegenüber, von denen jedes in der neuen Gesellschaft repräsentiert sein wollte. Fritz Johnston, C.I.-Verantwortlicher bei McDonnell Douglas, fragte, ob ich das vorhandene Symbol der Firma überarbeiten könne. Er erwarte von mir eine Lösung der visuellen Probleme (das Symbol sähe «wie eine Rakete aus, die auf ein Flugzeug abgefeuert wird», behauptete er), und gleichzeitig sollte

*__Rick Eiber__ aus Seattle, Washington, ist ein international anerkannter Spezialist für C.I.-Programme und Markenauftritte. Er ist Autor/Redakteur des bei Graphis Press erschienenen Buches World Trademarks: 100 Years und Mitglied der Alliance Graphique Internationale (AGI). Seine Arbeiten haben international grosse Anerkennung gefunden, was sich durch hunderte von Auszeichnungen und Veröffentlichungen manifestiert.*

es sich mit dem vorhandenen Boeing-Logo vereinbaren lassen. In dem neuen Symbol umkreist das Raumelement jetzt den «Globus», und die abgewandelte Flugzeugform kann entweder als kommerzieller Jet gesehen werden, der sich von links nach rechts bewegt, oder als eine Militärmaschine, die auf einen zukommt. Die Elemente unterstützten die Orientierung der meisten Firmenbereiche in Richtung Flugzeugbau, wobei gleichzeitig vorhandene Bestandteile der bisher bestehenden C.I.s eingebaut wurden. Der Auftritt entsprach der von Boeings Chairman Phil Condit formulierten Haltung: «Eine Firma, eine Vision». Dies trug zur Harmonisierung der beiden verschiedenen Unternehmenskulturen bei und reduzierte die Kosten für die Umwandlung bzw. den Übergang. Und wie wir alle wissen, ist das Einsparen von Kosten noch jeder Firma sehr lieb.

Auf dem globablen Markt unserer Zeit führen Fusionen und Übernahmen zu neuen, grossen, finanziell starken und visuell anspruchsvollen Firmeneinheiten, die die Latte für jedermann ständig höher anlegen – wobei sie es kleinen oder neuen Firmen schwer machen, überhaupt einen Fuss in die Arena zu setzen. Ein Logo ist eines der effektivsten Mittel, die ein Geschäftsführer einsetzen kann, um die Voraussetzungen zur Teilnahme am Spiel etwas auszugleichen. Ein einziges, mutiges graphisches Zeichen kann einer Firma, die mitspielen möchte, sofortige Anerkennung einbringen, egal ob sie alt oder ganz neu ist. Der ehemalige Chef von British Rail formulierte das so: «Design ist sichtbar gemachte Intelligenz.» Tatsächlich bedeutet ein hervorragendes Logo die visuelle Darstellung einer Firma. Und das ist immer und überall in geschäftlicher Hinsicht sinnvoll und vernünftig.

## Un bon logo c'est bon pour les affaires: Rick Eiber

**Coup d'œil rétrospectif: IBM et Westinghouse.** Par expérience, dès que l'on parle d'identité institutionnelle et de succès en affaires et que la conversation commence à s'échauffer, quelques secondes suffisent pour que l'un des interlocuteurs évoque les légendaires réalisations du regretté Paul Rand. Mais commençons par le début, soit par les deux programmes d'identité institutionnelle que le célèbre designer a conçus pour IBM et Westinghouse, deux références en la matière. Le programme réalisé pour IBM dans les années 50 ouvrit de toutes nouvelles perspectives. Paul Rand développa dans le cadre du programme original d'innombrables variations de logo, les unes plus époustouflantes que les autres. Symbolisant l'efficacité et la rapidité, une de ces versions accrocheuses barrée de rayures reliait les trois lettres du fabricant, dont les formes paraissaient impossibles à associer de prime abord. Il déclina ce logo dans deux versions, une fois avec 8 rayures et une fois avec 13 rayures, la dernière étant destinée à des documents officiels comme des contrats. Une nuance de bleu fut désignée sous le nom d'IBM Blue qui, suite à son application étendue et constante, valut bientôt à la société le surnom de «Big Blue». Si l'on passe maintenant aux années 90, on se rend compte que le logo IBM original a non seulement conservé toutes ses caractéristiques et son intégrité, mais qu'il est traité avec le plus profond respect tant par son propriétaire que par les hommes d'affaires qui connaissent la valeur d'un tel emblème. Voilà un logo connu et reconnu dans le monde entier, qui a prouvé qu'un bon design, c'est bon pour les affaires.

Pour 50'000 dollars US – somme aujourd'hui dérisoire qui ferait sourire plus d'un designer –, Rand créa en 1960 le logo intemporel «W» pour Westinghouse. Il modifia le symbole «W» souligné qui existait déjà en plaçant de petites boules sur les extrémités pour symboliser, selon toute évidence, un réacteur. A ce sujet, il est intéressant de se référer à l'avant-propos de son manuel d'identification graphique où il déclarait: «Westinghouse a porté son choix sur un programme de design à long terme... Avant que ce design n'ait une quelconque signification pour nos clients, il est impératif que tous les collaborateurs à tous les niveaux de la hiérarchie reconnaissent et comprennent sa finalité.» D'instinct, Rand semblait avoir saisi que, sans cette compréhension, un programme de design n'est rien.

Le «W» de Paul Rand demeure le symbole clé du programme de design graphique de Westinghouse. Les autres éléments incluaient une seule couleur pour l'entreprise, une typographie et la griffe de l'entreprise réalisée avec cette famille de caractères inédite. Le premier investissement de la société Westinghouse a rapporté d'énormes dividendes: les postes de l'actif de la société-mère dans le domaine de la propriété intellectuelle ont augmenté de plusieurs millions de dollars depuis!

**Le design de logos aujourd'hui: Microsoft et Boeing.** Lorsque les responsables de Microsoft m'ont chargé de revisiter leur logo, ils ont commencé par m'expliquer pourquoi l'ancienne version ne leur plaisait pas: «Le logo est illisible quand on l'imprime en négatif sur une couleur primaire ou qu'on le réduit à un petit format» – deux inconvénients majeurs lorsqu'un logo doit trouver une

*Basé à Seattle, Washington,* **Rick Eiber** *est un spécialiste mondialement connu dans les domaines de l'identité institutionnelle et du management de marque. Auteur et éditeur de* World Trademarks: 100 Years *qui paraît chez Graphis Press, il est également membre de l'Alliance Graphique Internationale (AGI). Ses travaux lui ont apporté une estime internationale qui lui a valu des centaines de distinctions et de nombreuses parutions dans divers publications.*

large application et être reconnaissable partout. Le fruit de mon travail qui dura une année entière déboucha notamment sur une série de maquettes pour des publications et un vaste code-couleurs destiné à tous les segments d'activité de la société. Pour Microsoft, il était clair qu'une identité visuelle devait reposer sur une nomenclature. Le fabricant utilisa donc son nom pour chaque produit, Microsoft Word par exemple, à la fois un logo, une identité et un nom. (A ce sujet, j'aimerais encore ajouter que j'aurais préféré être payé en actions: leur valeur a quadruplé depuis tandis qu'avec mes dollars, mon pouvoir d'achat ne cesse de baisser!)

Il y a douze ans, alors que je travaillais déjà pour une compagnie aérienne, Boeing m'a confié, en ma qualité de consultant en identité visuelle, la conception d'un programme pour la société canadienne deHaviland, dernière acquisition de l'époque. J'ai expliqué à mes commanditaires que nous n'obtiendrions pas grand-chose si chacune des compagnies poursuivait ses activités sous sa propre identité et un nom distinct. Et à moins que Boeing ne fasse le ménage, il n'y aurait pas de programme du tout. En analysant la nomenclature et le matériel, nous sommes arrivés à une solution partielle, qui devait nous renseigner sur la manière de résoudre les problèmes. C'est ainsi qu'au cours de ses 75 ans d'existence, la société passa son premier contrat portant sur un programme d'identité institutionnelle.

La fusion récente de Boeing avec McDonnell Douglas nous confronta à une tâche autrement plus complexe. Nous nous trouvions face à deux poids lourds qui voulaient tous deux être représentés dans la nouvelle société. Fritz Johnston, responsable de l'identité institutionnelle chez McDonnell Douglas, me demanda de retravailler le symbole de la compagnie. Il attendait de moi que je résolve d'une part les problèmes visuels – le symbole, selon lui, ressemblait à «un missile propulsé contre un avion» – et, d'autre part, que le résultat soit compatible avec le logo de Boeing. Sur le nouveau symbole, l'élément spatial effectue une rotation autour du «globe», et la forme modifiée de l'avion évoque à la fois un jet commercial qui vole de gauche à droite et un appareil militaire qui fonce sur nous. Les éléments utilisés reprennent les principaux segments d'activité de l'aéronautique tout en intégrant des caractéristiques des identités préexistantes. La nouvelle identité reflète parfaitement l'attitude préconisée par Phil Condit, directeur de Boeing: «Une compagnie, une vision». Ce concept a largement contribué à l'harmonisation des deux cultures d'entreprise et à la réduction des frais de transition. Et comme chacun sait, le vœu le plus cher de toute entreprise, c'est bien d'économiser de l'argent.

A l'époque de la globalisation, les fusions et acquisitions donnent naissance à des géants aux moyens financiers énormes et à l'identité élaborée, qui placent la barre toujours plus haut et rendent la tâche d'autant plus difficile pour les sociétés modestes ou nouvellement fondées désireuses de se lancer dans l'arène. Pour un directeur d'entreprise, le logo est le meilleur moyen de redistribuer les cartes et de se donner ainsi les moyens de remplir les conditions de participation au jeu. Un seul signe graphique audacieux peut apporter la reconnaissance immédiate à une société qui aspire à rentrer dans la partie, peu importe qu'elle soit jeune ou établie. L'ancien directeur de British Rail l'a formulé ainsi: «Le design, c'est un signe d'intelligence devenu visible.» En effet, un logo bien conçu rend une société visible. Et c'est ce qui donne un sens aux affaires, partout, à chaque instant.

Logo Design 1999

*(this page)*
Design Firm:
Oakley Design Studios
Art Director, Designer, Illustrator:
Tim Oakley
Client:
Doug Baldwin

*(opposite, first from top)*
Design Firm:
Nike, Inc (in house)
Art Director, Designer:
Jeff Weithman
Illustrator:
David Gill
Client:
Nike, Inc.

*(second from top)*
Design Firm:
Sandstrom Design
Designer:
Steve Sandstrom
Client:
Radioland

*(third from top)*
Creative Director:
John Lee
Art Director, Designer:
David Healy
Client:
Mezzina/ Brown Inc.

*(fourth from top)*
Design Firm:
Oakley Design Studios
Creative Director, Art Director, Illustrator:
Tim Oakley
Client:
Meyer Projection Systems

*(bottom)*
Design Firm:
Goodby, Silverstein & Partners
Creative Director:
Rich Silverstein, Paul Curan
Art Director:
Keith Anderson
Illustrator:
Bruce Hutchison
Client:
Goodby, Silverstein & Partners

nike

Radioland

CAMEL
1913 1998
85TH ANNIVERSARY

Goodby, Silverstein & Partners

*(this page)*
Design Firm: RBMM/ The Richards Group
Client: Luis Mejio

*(opposite, first from top)*
Client: JSA Inc.
Design Firm: Intelligent Design Enforcement Agency
Creative Director, Designer: Thomas Puckett

*(second from top)*
Design Firm: Art Force Studio
Art Director, Designer, Illustrator: Halasi Zoltan
Client: Victor Invest KFT

*(third from top)*
Design Firm: Korn Design
Art Director: Denise Korn
Designer: Javier Cortés
Client: McMahon Architects

*(fourth from top)*
Design Firm: BBV
Art Director: Michael Baviera
Designer: Siegrun Nuber
Client: Erecheinungsbild Architekturbüro

*(this page, top)*
Design Firm:
Mires
Design
Client:
The
Copeland
Reis
Agency

*(bottom)*
Design Firm:
Pennebaker
LMC
Creative Director:
Jeffrey McKay
Art Director,
Designer:
Greg Valdez
Client:
Words,
Pictures,
& Sounds

*(opposite, top)*
Design Firm:
Tim Tucker
Images
Art Director,
Designer:
Tim Tucker

*(bottom)*
Design Firm:
On Target
Advertising
Client:
Neal
Tabachnick,
On the One, Inc.

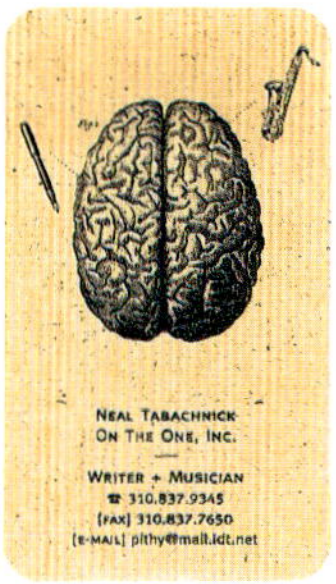
Neal Tabachnick
On The One, Inc.
Writer + Musician
☎ 310.837.9345
[fax] 310.837.7650
[e-mail] pithy@mail.idt.net

*(this spread)*
Design Firm: Design Hoch Drei
Designers: Sabine Arenz, Diethard Keppler, Wolfram Schaeffer, Kai Twelbeck
Client: Mercedes-Benz AG, Press Department

*(this page, first from top)*
Design Firm: Sandstrom Design
Designer: Steve Sandstrom
Client: Go Spot Go Carwash

*(second from top)*
Design Firm: The Designory Inc.
Creative Director: Tim Meraz
Designer: Paul Ison
Client: Mercedes-Benz North America

*(third from top)*
Design Firm: Hasan & Partners
Art Director, Designer, Illustrator: Kimmo Kivilahti
Client: Brumm Brumm Harley Service

*(fourth from top)*
Design Firm: Swieter Design U.S.
Creative Director: John Swieter
Designer: Mark Ford
Client: Classified Ventures

*(bottom)*
Design Firm: Sandstrom Design
Designer: Steve Sandstrom
Client: Nissan

*(opposite)*
Design Firm: Gerstman & Meyers Inc.
Creative Director: Juan Concepcion
Designer: Susan Payne
Client: Sargento

SARGENTO®
SARGENTO
NYLINT
NYLINT
NYLINT
NYLINT
NYLINT

*(this page)*
Design Firm: Mires Design
Creative Director, Art Director: José Serrano
Designers: José Serrano, Miguel Perez
Illustrator: Tracy Sabin
Client: Gary's Hot Rods

*(opposite, first from top)*
Design Firm: Graco Advertising Dept.
Art Director: Gary Schmidt
Client: Graco Automotive Division

*(second from top)*
Design Firm: Alan Chan Design Co.
Art Director: Alan Chan
Designer: Alan Chan, Miu Choy
Client: Collectors' Club

*(third from top)*
Design Firm: Mires Design Inc.
Creative Director, Art Director, Designer: José Serrano
Illustrator: Tracy Sabin
Client: Hot Rod Hell

*(bottom)*
Design Firm: Sayles Graphic Design
Art Director, Designer, Illustrator: John Sayles
Client: Beckley Imports

SHAUN MCCARTHY

KAOS

A
CUT
AHEAD
HAIR SALON

WHIPPER
SNAPPERS
hair squad

*(opposite, first from top)*
Design Firm: Brainstorm Inc.
Creative Director: Chuck Johnson
Art Director: Jeff Dey
Designers: Jeff Dey, Chuck Johnson, Wayne Geyer
Illustrators: Chuck Johnson, Jeff Dey
Client: Shaun McCarthy Salon

*(second from top)*
Design Firm: GSD&M
Designer: Brett Stiles
Client: Kids Are Our Specialty

*(third from top)*
Design Firm: Sayles Graphic Design
Art Director, Designer: John Sayles
Client: A Cut Ahead

*(fourth from top)*
Design Firm: Duffy Design
Creative Director: Joe Duffy
Art Director: Kobe
Designers, Illustrators: Kobe, Jason Strong
Client: Avant

*(bottom)*
Design Firm: Brainstorm Inc.
Creative Director: Chuck Johnson
Art Directors: Jeff Dey
Designers: Chuck Johnson, Jeff Dey, Wayne Geyer
Client: Whipper Snapper Hair Squad

*(this page)*
Design Firm: Duffy Design
Creative Director: Joe Duffy
Art Director: Kobe
Designers: Kobe, Dan Olson
Client: Retail Concepts, Inc.

HOPPERS
GRILL & BREWING CO.

BREWING
SINCE
MACKINAW
1997
COMPANY

*(opposite, first, second from top)*
Design Firm:
HM Design
Art Director:
Dave Malone
Designers:
Dave Malone,
Reed Anderson
Client:
Sizzling Platters,
Inc.

*(third from top)*
Design Firm:
May & Co.
Creative Director,
Art Director:
Doug May
Designer:
Chris Rovillo
Client:
Martin Sinkoff
Wines, Inc.

*(fourth from top)*
Design Firm:
Nielsen Design
Group
Art Director,
Designer:
Tim Nielsen
Client:
Mackinaw
Brewing Co.

*(bottom)*
Design Firm:
Sandstrom
Design
Designer:
Sally Morrow
Illustrators:
Sally Morrow,
Janée Warren
Client:
Portland
Brewing Co.

*(this page)*
Design Firm:
Ross Patrick
Los Angeles
Art Director,
Designer:
Ross Patrick
Client:
Schlessinger
Bros.

RACCOON
RIVER
BREWING
CO.

*(opposite)*
Design Firm:
Sayles Graphic Design
Art Director, Designer:
John Sayles
Client:
Raccoon River Brewing Co.

*(this page, first from top)*
Design Firm:
Phoenix Creative
Creative Director:
Eric Thoelke
Art Director, Designer:
Kathy Wilkinson
Illustrator:
Raphael Montoliu
Client:
Anheuser-Busch Specialty Brewing Group

*(second from top)*
Design Firm:
Mires Design, Inc.
Art Director, Designer:
John Ball
Illustrator:
Jim Staunton
Client:
Temecula Valley Wine Country

*(third from top)*
Design Firm:
Planet Design Company
Client:
Angelic Brewing Co.

*(fourth from top)*
Design Firm:
Thompson & Company
Creative Director, Designer:
Rick Baptist
Art Director:
Trace Hallowell
Photographer:
Davidson & Company
Client:
Delta Beverage Group

*(bottom)*
Design Firm:
Compass Design
Art Director:
Mitchell Lindgren
Designers:
Mitchell Lindgren, Tom Arthur, Rich McGowen
Illustrator:
Cindy Lindgren
Client:
Buckin' Bass Brewing Co.

TELEMARKETING
Bell

Disney Online

*(opposite, first from top)*
Design Firm:
Art Force Studio
Art Director, Designer:
Simon Attila
Client:
Nautica Marketing and Design Consulting

*(second from top)*
Design Firm:
Schumacher WA
Designer:
Sabine Koehler
Client:
Kinderkram Kommunikation

*(third from top)*
Design Firm:
EAT Advertising & Design
Creative Director:
Patrice Eilts Jobe
Art Director, Designer:
Peggy Reilly
Client:
Micromedia, Inc.

*(fourth from top)*
Design Firm:
Think New Ideas
Creative Director:
Larry Kopald
Art Director, Designer:
Ken Loh
Client:
Think New Ideas

*(bottom)*
Design Firm:
Disney Online
Art Director, Designer:
David Vogler
Illustrator:
Ben Luce
Client:
The Walt Disney Company

*(this page)*
Design Firm:
Coley Porter Bell
Creative Director:
Alli Mignel
Art Director:
Stephen Bell
Designers:
Stephen Bell, Sonya Frick

*(opposite, first from top)*
Design Firm: Zimmermann Crowe Design
Art Director: Dennis Crowe
Designers: Angie Wang, Dennis Crowe
Illustrator: Geof Kern
Client: Sense8 Corporation

*(second from top)*
Design Firm: Meta-4 Incorporated
Creative Director, Designer, Illustrator: Meta-4
Client: Light House Communications

VANALT

*(third from top)*
Design Firm: Michael Schwab Studio
Art Director: Hugh Flanigan
Designer: Michael Schwab
Client: American Online

*(fourth from top)*
Design Firm: Joseph Rattan Design
Art Director: Joseph Rattan
Designer, Illustrator: Diana McKnight
Client: Marketing Vision

*(bottom)*
Design Firm: RBMM/ The Richards Group
Art Director, Designer: Pamela Chang
Client: Talktech

*(previous spread, right page; left)*
Design Firm:
Haley Johnson Design Co.
Designer, Illustrator:
Richard Boynton
Client:
Tea for Two

*(middle)*
Design Firm:
VanAlt Group, Inc.
Creative Directors, Designers:
John Homs, Robin Schroeder
Illustrator:
Scott Wright
Client:
VanAlt Group, Inc.

*(right)*
Design Firm:
Swieter Design U.S.
Creative Director:
John Swieter
Designer:
Mark Ford
Client:
Swieter Design U.S.

*(this page)*
Design Firm:
Brandon Murphy
Art Director, Designer:
Brandon Murphy
Client:
Mobile Internet Studio

*(opposite)*
Design Firm:
Art Technology Group
Client:
Dynamo

*(opposite, first from top)*
Design Firm: neue reklame
Creative Directors: Markus Heinback, Carsten Strübbe
Client: Ollas Concepts

*(second from top)*
Design Firm: VSA Partners, Inc.
Client: Xsite Internet Provider

*(third from top)*
Design Firm: Pennebaker Design
Art Director, Designer, Illustrator: Greg Valdez
Client: VISTA Corp.

*(bottom)*
Design Firm: Studio d'Design
Client: Concierge Software

*(this page, top)*
Design Firm: Frazier Design
Art Director, Designer: Craig Frazier
Client: Xaos Tools, Inc.

*(middle)*
Design Firm: Gill Fishman Associates
Art Director: Gill Fishman
Designer: Tammy Torrey
Illustrator: David Taylor
Client: Organic Systems

ORGANIC
SYSTEMS

*(bottom)*
Design Firm: Drive Communciations
Art Director, Designer: Michael Graziolo
Client: Vuepoint, Inc.

*(this page, top)*
Design Firm:
Swieter Design
U.S.
Creative Director:
John Swieter
Designer:
Julie Poth
Client:
Aeroware

*(middle)*
Design Firm:
Supon
Design
Group
Art Director,
Designer:
Andrew
Dolan
Client:
Paradise
Wild

*(bottom)*
Design Firm:
RBBM/
The Richards
Group
Art Director,
Designer,
Illustrator: Luis
Acevedo
Client:
Blitz
Software

*(opposite)*
Design Firm:
Hornall
Anderson
Design Works
Art Director,
Designer:
Jack Anderson
Client:
Nextlink
Corp.

NEXTLINK

*(this page)*
Design Firm: Pennebaker. LMC
Creative Director: Jeffrey McKay
Art Director, Designer: David Lerch
Client: Western Atlas, Smart 3D

*(opposite)*
Design Firm: Spangler Associates, Inc.
Creative Director: Allen Woodard
Designer, Illustrator: Michael Conners
Client: Mainstar

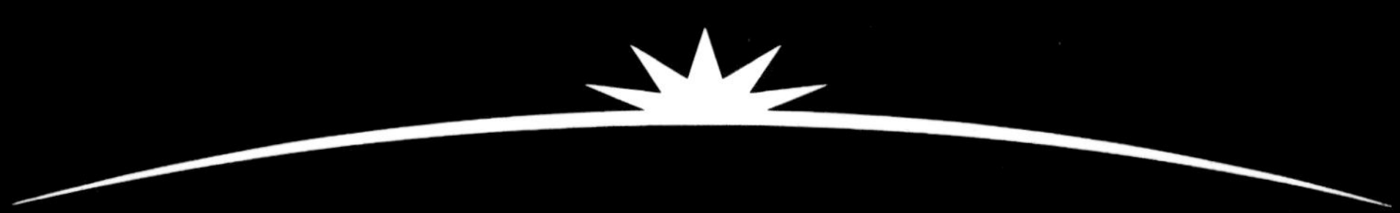

*(opposite)*
Design Firm:
Baumann &
Peyer
Art Director,
Designer:
Brigitte
Bohnen
Client:
Max
Vogelsang
AG

FOUNDED IN 1878
BARRICK
ROOFING
&
SHEET METAL
· INC. ·

*(this page)*
Design Firm:
Sayles
Graphic
Design
Art Director,
Designer,
Illustrator:
John Sayles
Client:
Barrick
Roofing

*(this page)*
Design Firm:
Lauren Smith
Design
Art Director,
Designer:
Lauren Smith
Client:
Williams
Construction

*(opposite)*
Design Firm:
Alternativ Studio
Art Director,
Designer:
Peter Vajda
Client:
Aedificium

*(this page)*
Design Firm: Linden Design/ Logoguy
Designer: Stephen Linden
Client: Symplectic Engineering Corporation

*(opposite, first from top)*
Design Firm: White Design, Inc.
Client: Barrington

*(second from top)*
Design Firm: Dreier Design
Client: Kodiak Consulting

*(third from top)*
Design Firm: Linden Design/ Logoguy
Designer: Stephen Linden
Client: Harold Hedelman

*(fourth from top)*
Design Firm: Michael Kelly Designs
Art Director, Designer: Michael Kelly
Client: Strategic Resources, Inc.

*(bottom)*
Design Firm: The Weller Institute for the Cure of Design
Art Director, Designer: Don Weller
Client: The Praxis Institute

*(this page)*
Design Firm:
Ron Kellum
Inc.
Art Director,
Designer:
Ron Kellum
Client:
Boiling
Point

*(opposite)*
Design Firm:
Cronan
Design
Creative Director:
Michael Cronan
Client:
Principals.com

*(opposite)*
Design Firm:
Tor Petterson
& Partners
Ltd.
Art Director:
Tor Petterson
Designers:
Tor Pettersen,
Craig Johnson,
Joanna Pettersen
Client:
Enterprise
Oil Plc



*(this page)*
Art Director,
Designer,
Illustrator:
Kyosti Varis

*(this page)*
Design Firm:
Supon Design Group, Inc.
Art Director, Designer:
Andrew Dolan
Client:
Creative Strategies, Inc.

*(opposite, first from top)*
Design Firm:
Frank D'Astolfo Design
Art Director, Designer:
Frank D'Astolfo
Client:
Alimenterics

*(second from top)*
Design Firm:
MacNab Design
Art Director, Designer:
Maggie McNab
Client:
Energy Related Devices

*(third from top)*
Design Firm:
Hornall Anderson Design Works, Inc.
Art Director:
Jack Anderson
Designers:
Jack Anderson, Jana Wilson, Lisa Cerveny, Julie Keenen
Client:
XactData Corp.

*(fourth from top)*
Design Firm:
Richards/Weithman
Art Directors, Designers:
Dan Richards, Jeff Weithman
Client:
The Baby Jogger Company

*(bottom)*
Design Firm:
Deep Design
Art Director:
Rick Grimsley
Designers:
Rick Grimsley, Mark Steingruber
Client: UPS Worldwide Logistics

*(this page)*
Design Firm:
Nike, Inc.
Client:
Nike, Inc.

*(opposite, top)*
Design Firm:
The Design
Company of
San Francisco
Client:
Benevia

*(middle)*
Design Firm:
Mires Design
Creative Director:
John Ball
Designers:
John Ball,
Kathy
Carpenter-
Moore
Illustrator:
Dan Thoner
Client:
Business
Communications
Network

*(bottom)*
Design Firm:
Essex Two
Art Director,
Designer,
Illustrator:
Joseph
Michael Essex
Client:
Motorola

BENEVIA

BUSINESS COMMUNICATIONS
SAN DIEGO NETWORK CALIFORNIA

TLC

*(this page)*
Design Firm:
Signal
Communications
Art Director,
Designer:
Scott Severson
Client:
Foresight

*(opposite)*
Design Firm:
Doo Kim
Design
Art Director:
Doo Kim
Designers:
Dongil Lee,
Seung
Hee Lee
Client:
Korea
International
Trade
Association

KITA
KOREA
INTERNATIONAL
TRADE
ASSOCIATION

HUFFY

*(opposite, first from top)*
Design Firm: Devcom
Creative Director: Steven Gross
Client: Sarnoff Bio Com Group

*(second from top)*
Design Firm: Brainstrom Inc.
Art Director, Designer, Illustrator: Chuck Johnson
Client: Deke Hayes

*(third from top)*
Design Firm: Pentagram Design
Art Director: Kit Hinrichs
Designer: Jackie Foshaug
Client: The Gymboree Corporation

*(fourth from top)*
Design Firm: Huffy Bicycles Design Center
Creative Director: Bill Rieger
Art Director, Designer: Greg Fehrenbach
Client: Huffy BMX

*(bottom)*
Design Firm: Shigeo Katsuoka Design Studio
Art Director, Designer: Shigeo Katsuoka
Client: Meiji Mutual Life Insurance

*(this page)*
Design Firm: Frankfurt Balkind Partners
Client: Hallmark Entertainment

[WORLDWIDE OPERATIONS]

[MISSION STATEMENT]

[STRATEGIC INITIATIVES]

[VALUES]

[ARCHITECTURAL DIRECTION]

[COMPONENTS]

*(opposite)*
Design Firm: Earl Gee Design
Art Director: Earl Gee
Designers: Earl Gee, Fani Chung
Client: Sun Microsystems, Inc.

*(this page)*
Design Firm: Rickabaugh Graphics
Client: The Walker Group

*(this page)*
Design Firm:
Sandstrom
Design
Art Director,
Designer:
Steve
Sandstrom
Client:
Artsy Fartsy
Productions

PVFFT.

ARTSY · FARTSY
PRODVCTIONS

*(opposite)*
Design Firm:
Cronan Design
Art Director,
Designer,
Illustrator:
Michael
Cronan
Designer:
Anthony Yell
Client:
Engineering
Animation
Interactive

EAI

INTERACTIVE

EAI

SOFTWARE

EAI

ANIMATION

EAI

VISUALIZATION

*(opposite, first from top)*
Design Firm: Michael Schwab Design
Art Directors: David Payne, Darren Briggs
Designer: Michael Schwab
Client: Cannonball Graphics

*(second from top)*
Design Firm: Vanderbyl Design
Art Director, Designer, Illustrator: Michael Vanderbyl
Client: Robb Murray & Company

*(third from top)*
Design Firm: Sibley/Peteet Design
Creative Director: Rex Peteet
Client: Brittany Hartley, Professional Ballerina

*(bottom)*
Art Directors, Designers: Kris Murphy, Brandon Murphy
Illustrator: Kris Murphy
Client: Black Rhino Graphics

*(this page)*
Design Firm: Frazier Design
Art Director, Designer: Craig Frazier
Client: Magico

*(this page, top)*
Design Firm: Insight Design Communications
Art Directors, Designers: Sherrie Holdeman, Tracy Holdeman
Client: Virtual Celebrity Productions

*(middle)*
Design Firm: Insight Design Communications
Art Directors, Designers: Sherrie Holdeman, Tracy Holdeman
Client: The Stables

*(bottom)*
Design Firm: Insight Design Communications
Art Directors, Designers: Sherrie Holdeman, Tracy Holdeman
Client: Fresh Paint

*(opposite)*
Design Firm: Zamboo
Designers: Dave Zambotti, Becca Bootes
Client: Creative Management Coordinators

MADISON GRAPHICS

ARTUSTRY
partnership

*(opposite, top)*
Design Firm:
Peter Good
Graphic Design
Art Director,
Designer,
Illustrator:
Peter Good
Client:
Custom
Covers

*(middle)*
Design Firm:
Madison
Graphics
Creative Director:
Stephen King
Art Director,
Designer:
Mike Romeo
Client:
Madison
Graphics

*(bottom)*
Design Firm:
Studio A
Art Director,
Designer:
Rachel
Allgood
Photographer:
Stasia Droze
Client:
Artustry
Partnership

*(this page, top)*
Design Firm:
Signal
Communications
Art Director,
Designer:
Scott Severson
Client:
Photo
Effects

*(middle)*
Design Firm:
Deep Design
Designers:
Rick Grimsley,
Lee Manis
Client:
LithoKrome

*(bottom)*
Design Firm:
Tracy Sabin
Graphic
Design
Art Director:
Tom Stacey
Photographer:
Tracy Sabin
Client:
The
Wordsmith

*(this page, top)*
Design Firm: Orbit Integrated
Art Director, Designer: Jack Harris
Illustrator: Joe Ski
Client: Orbit Integrated

*(bottom)*
Design Firm: Mires Design
Art Director, Designer: Mike Brower
Illustrators: Tracy Sabin, Miguel Perez
Client: M.G. Swing Co.

Livestock™

SINCE 1993
M.G. SWING COMPANY
Painting Contractors

*(opposite, top)*
Design Firm: Orbit Integrated
Art Director, Designer: Jack Harris
Client: Visual Logic

*(bottom)*
Design Firm: RBMM
Art Director, Designer: Tom Nynas
Client: Cat Jugglers

*(this page, top, middle)*
Design Firm:
Nielsen Design
Group
Art Director:
Tim Nielsen
Designer:
Emily Mitchell
Illustrator:
Glen Wolff
Client:
Folgarelli's Market

*(bottom)*
Design Firm:
Shook Design
Group, Inc.
Art Director:
Ginger Riley
Designer,
Illustrator:
Jeffrey Camillo
Client:
Fuel Pizza Cafe

*(opposite)*
Design Firm:
Muller & Co.
Art Director:
Susan Wilson
Designers:
Dave Swearingen,
Kelly Baker
Client:
Gambucci's

ITALIAN
GAMBUCCI'S

*(this page)*
Design Firm:
DogStar
Client:
Typhoon
Restaurant

*(opposite, first from top)*
Design Firm:
Felix
Sockwell Creative
Art Director,
Designer:
Felix Sockwell
Client:
Deep Sushi

*(second from top)*
Design Firm:
Nielsen Design
Group
Art Director:
Tim Nielsen
Designer:
Emily Mitchell
Client:
Stone House
Bread

*(third from top)*
Design Firm:
Pentagram
Design, Inc.
Art Director:
Kit Hinrichs
Designer:
Jackie Foshaug
Client:
Columbus
Salame, Inc.

*(fourth from top)*
Design Firm:
Mires Design, Inc.
Creative Director,
Designer:
José Serrano
Illustrator:
Tracy Sabin
Client: Pepsi

*(bottom)*
Design Firm:
Keith Harris
Package Design
Art Director,
Designer,
Illustrator:
Keith Harris
Client:
Kaffeerösterei
Tempelmann

DEEP SUSHI · DEEP ELLUM ·

REAL LEELANAU SOURDOUGH

COLUMBUS SALAME COMPANY

THE INSTITUTE FOR BEVERAGE RESEARCH

BREMER · STOLZ ·

*(this page, first from top)*
Design Firm: Becker Design
Art Director, Designer: Neil Becker
Client: Latte LaLa

*(second from top)*
Design Firm: Sandstrom Design
Art Director, Designer: Steve Sandstrom
Client: Tazo

*(third from top)*
Design Firm: Zoom
Art Director: Asko Künnap
Client: Kuumärk Ltd.

*(bottom)*
Design Firm: Mitchell & Company
Creative Director: Vyto Bendoraitis
Art Director, Designer: Mitchell Hock-Henningsen
Illustrator: Evangelia Philippidis
Client: Mitchell & Company

*(opposite)*
Design Firm: Sandstrom Design
Art Director, Designer, Illustrator: Steve Sandstrom
Client: Tazo

THE REINCARNATION of TEA
Envy
GREEN TEA & HERBS
TAZO
The sharp fresh taste of green teas balanced with notes of lemon, mint and desire.
Net Wt. 2oz.
(56 grams)

TAZO
Simply Red
Passion Potion
[tea & juice]
The exotic taste of passionfruit mixed with refreshing microbrewed green tea.
16 fluid ounces (473ml)
Basic Black
[iced tea]
A microbrewed classic black tea with a light, natural sweetness.
16 fluid ounces (473ml)

*(opposite)*
Design Firm: Pentagram Design Ltd.
Art Directors: Alan Dye, Tom Lloyd, Stuart Oldridge
Designers: Daniel Weil, John Greenfield
Client: Granada Hospitality

*(this page, top)*
Design Firm: Signal Communications
Art Director, Designer: Scott Severson
Client: Teaism

*(middle)*
Design Firm: Signal Communications
Art Director, Designer: Scott Severson
Client: Starland Cafe

*(bottom)*
Design Firm: Signal Communications
Art Director, Designer: Scott Severson
Client: Cafe Bethesda

*(next spread, left; top)*
Design Firm: Sayles Graphic Design
Art Director, Designer: John Sayles
Client: Capital Club

*(middle; right page)*
Design Firm: Planet Design Co.
Art Directors: Dana Lytle, Kevin Wade
Designers: Kevin Wade, Martha Craeittinger
Client: Candinas

*(bottom)*
Design Firm: Sayles Graphic Design
Art Director, Designer: John Sayles
Client: Chicago Dog and Deli

CAPITAL CLUB

DES MOINES IOWA

C

CHICAGO DOG AND DELI

CANDINAS CHOCOLATES
CANDINAS CHOCOLATIER
2pc.

EVEN SO BAKING CO.
RISE & SHINE

CITY DELI

Luigi's
DINER

WILD ALASKAN SALMON
AQUACUISINE

*(opposite, first from top)*
Design Firm:
Pattee Design
Designers:
Steve Patee,
Trenton Burd
Client:
Cabo San
Lucas
Restaurant

*(second from top)*
Design Firm:
Principia
Graphica
Client:
Even So
Baking

*(third from top)*
Design Firm:
Sommese
Design
Designers:
Larry Sommese,
Kristin Breslin
Sommese
Client:
City Deli

*(fourth from top)*
Design Firm:
Planet Design
Co.
Art Director:
Dana Lytle
Designer:
Ben Hirby
Client:
Food Fight

*(bottom)*
Design Firm:
Michael Schwab
Design
Art Director:
Doug Gilmour
Designer,
Illustrator:
Michael Schwab
Client:
AquaCuisine

*(this page)*
Design Firm:
Deep Design
Art Director:
Rick Grimsley
Designers:
Rick Grimsley,
Mark Steingruber
Client:
Honey Baked
Ham Co. of
Georgia

MEXTREME

BROWER
BAR & GRILL
EST. 1991 DEL MAR, CA

GOSTILNA
od leta 1778
Pri Kuklju

CARRY HOME
Bob Evans
KITCHEN

Redeye
GRILL

*(opposite, first from top)*
Design Firm: Mires Design Inc.
Art Director: Jose Serrano
Designers: Jose Serrano, Jeff Samaripa
Illustrator: Miguel Perez
Client: Food Group

*(second from top)*
Design Firm: Simple Green Design
Art Director, Designer, Illustrator: Mike Brower
Clients: Mike & Tabi Brower

*(third from top)*
Design Firm: KROG
Art Director, Designer: Edi Berk
Client: Gostilna Pri Kuklju

*(fourth from top)*
Design Firm: Chute Gerdeman, Inc.
Creative Director: Susan Hessler
Designer: Tim Frame
Client: Bob Evans Farms

*(bottom)*
Design Firm: The Sloan Group
Art Director: Cliff Sloan
Designer: Janet Eusebio
Client: Cafe Concepts

*(this page)*
Design Firm: Felix Sockwell Creative
Art Director, Designer: Felix Sockwell
Client: TC Partnership

FINE BREADS IN THE EUROPEAN TRADITION
MADE FRESH IN THE KITCHENS AT BYERLY'S
ALL NATURAL
ARTISAN
BREAD
COMPANY
TRADE MARK

*(opposite)*
Design Firm:
Parachute
Designer:
Bob Upton
Client:
Byerlys

*(first from top)*
Design Firm:
Pamela Chang
Client:
All Wrapped Up/
International
Burritos

*(second from top)*
Design Firm:
Meta-4
Incorporated
Art Director,
Designer,
Illustrator:
Meta-4
Client:
Terra An
American
Bistro

*(third from top)*
Design Firm:
HIXO
Art Director:
Tom Poth
Designer:
Mike Hicks
Client:
Sweetish Hill
Bakery

*(fourth from top)*
Design Firm:
Little & Co.
Client:
Campiello

*(bottom)*
Design Firm:
Marketplace
Design
Creative Directors:
Richard Hill,
Colin Goodall
Client:
DJ's Baked
Potatoes

*(this page, top)*
Art Director:
Mary Lewis
Designers:
Nin Glaister,
Ann Marshall
Client:
Les Anges

*(middle)*
Design Firm:
Weiss, Whitten,
Stagliano
Client:
Buck's
County
Coffee

*(bottom)*
Design Firm:
Felix Sockwell
Creative
Art Director,
Designer:
Felix Sockwell
Client:
Hidden
Grounds

LES ANGES

*(opposite, top)*
Design Firm:
Millford vdB
Client:
Meneba

*(middle)*
Design Firm:
Cato Berro
Diseño
Designer:
Gonzalo Berro
Client:
Diavolvo
Restaurant

*(bottom)*
Design Firm:
Millford vdB
Client: Meneba

meneba
Laan

Diavolo

meneba
meneba
meneba
meneba

*(this page)*
Design Firm:
Alan Chan
Art Director,
Designer:
Alan Chan

*(opposite, first from top)*
Design Firm:
Schulte
Design
Art Director,
Designer:
Paul Schulte
Illustrator:
RJ Muna
Pictures
Client:
San Francisco
Ballet

*(second from top)*
Design Firm:
Signal
Communications
Art Director,
Designer:
JJ Chrystal
Client:
Nomads, Inc.

*(third from top)*
Design Firm:
Mires Design,
Inc.
Creative Director:
John Ball
Designers:
Miguel Perez,
John Ball
Illustrator:
Miguel Perez
Client:
California
Center
for the Arts

*(bottom)*
Design Firm:
Sibley/Peteet
Design
Designer:
Rex Peteet

65 YEARS
SAN FRANCISCO BALLET

NOMADS

CALIFORNIA CENTER FOR THE ARTS
ESCONDIDO

*(this page)*
Design Firm:
Troy M. Litten
Design
Art Director,
Designer,
Illustrator:
Troy M. Litten
Client:
Troy M. Litten

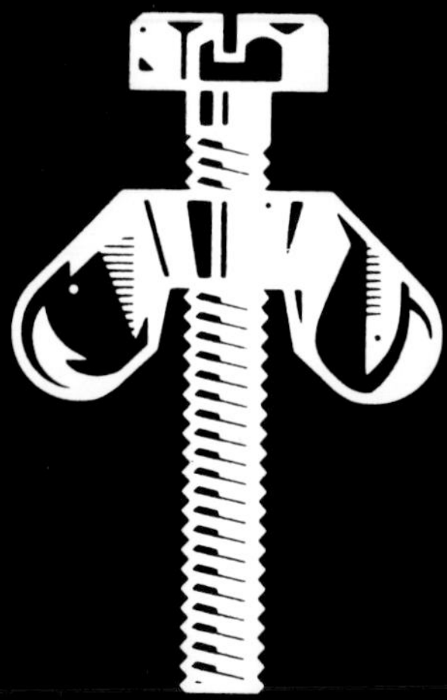

*(opposite)*
Design Firm:
Graphics &
Designing Inc.
Art Director,
Designer:
Toshihiro
Onimaru
Client: G & D
Management, Inc.

DRIVE

SAYLES GRAPHIC DESIGN

*(opposite, first from top)*
Design Firm: Swieter Design U.S.
Art Director, Designer: Mark Ford
Client: Swieter Design Interactive

*(second from top)*
Design Firm: Greteman Group
Art Director, Designer: James Strange
Client: Greteman Group

*(third from top)*
Design Firm: Drive Communications
Art Director, Designer: Michael Graziolo
Photographer: Michael Watson
Client: Drive Communications

*(fourth from top)*
Design Firm: Hat Nyugen Design
Art Director, Designer: Hat Nyugen
Client: Hat Nyugen Design

*(bottom)*
Design Firm: Sayles Graphic Design
Creative Director, Designer: John Sayles
Client: Sayles Graphic Design

*(this page)*
Design Firm: Gerard Huerta Design, Inc.
Art Director: TDC Board of Directors
Designer: Gerard Huerta
Illustrators: Gerard Huerta, Barbara Gibb
Client: Type Directors Club

*(this page)*
Design Firm:
Planet Design
Company
Client:
Planet Design
Company

*(opposite, first from top)*
Design Firm:
Charles Anderson
Design Co.
Art Director,
Designer:
Todd Hauswirth
Client:
Todd Hauswirth

*(second, fourth from top)*
Design Firm:
Imagination
Corp.
Art Director,
Designer:
Heather Gomes
Client:
Imagination
Corp.

*(third from top)*
Design Firm:
Royal Rocket
Studio
Art Director,
Designer,
Illustrator:
Kathi Zsolt
Client: Royal
Rocket Studio

*(bottom)*
Design Firm:
The Office
of Ted Fabella
Art Director,
Designer:
Tedd Fabella
Client:
The Office
of Ted Fabella

*(this page)*
Design Firm:
Dotzler
Creative Arts
Art Director:
Ray Dotzler
Designer:
Tim Grutsch
Client: Dotzler
Creative Arts

*(opposite)*
Design Firm:
Carmichael Lynch
Thorburn
Art Director:
Bill Thorburn
Designer:
Chad Hagen
Illustrators:
Chad Hagen,
David Schrimfe
Client: Carmichael
Lynch Thorburn

close
TESTED
COOL
ELECTRIC
FAITHFUL
PRIME
HERO
AUTO
Off
On
open
LOYAL-T
FEEL
LABOR
RESOURCE

OPEN SOCIETY ARCHIVES
AT CENTRAL EUROPEAN UNIVERSITY

FILM DOCUMENTS

SOUND DOCUMENTS

WRITTEN DOCUMENTS

*(opposite)*
Design Firm: Alternativ Studio
Art Director, Designer: Péter Vajda
Client: Open Society Archives

*(this page, left)*
Design Firm: Mires Design Inc.
Art Director, Designer: José A. Serrano
Illustrator: Mark Mattingly
Client: Hage Elementary

*(middle)*
Design Firm: Sackett Design Associates
Art Director, Designer: Mark Sackett
Illustrator: Calvin Patlon
Client: Firefighters in the Schools

*(right)*
Design Firm: Sibley/Peteet Design
Creative Director: Rex Peteet
Client: University of Texas/ MBA Program

*(this page)*
Design Firm:
Swieter Design
U.S
Art Director,
Designer:
Mark Ford
Client:
Young
Presidents'
Organization

*(opposite, first from top)*
Design Firm:
Pennebaker.
LMC
Client:
T.H. Rogers
Middle School

*(second from top)*
Design Firm:
RBMM
Art Director,
Designer:
Shayne
Washburn
Client:
First Baptist
Academy

*(third from top)*
Design Firm:
The Delor
Group
Art Directors:
Ken Delor,
Chris Enander
Designers:
Chris Enander,
Karen Boone
Illustrator:
Holly Stewart
Client:
USA Group

*(fourth from top)*
Design Firm:
Seran Design
Art Director,
Designer:
Sang Yoon
Client:
James Madison
University/
College of
Education and
Psychology

*(bottom)*
Design Firm:
Ann Bereron
Client:
University of
Illinois

*(this page)*
Design Firm:
Selbert Perkins
Design
Collaborative
Creative Director:
Robin Perkins
Designers:
John Lutz,
Mike Balint
Client: Chia Tai
Riverfest

*(opposite,
first from top)*
Design Firm:
Swieter Design
Art Director,
Designer:
John Swieter
Client:
Swieter Design
U.S.

*(second from top)*
Design Firm:
RBMM/
Richards Group
Art Director,
Designer:
Horacio Cobos
Illustrator:
Wayne Johnson
Client:
Amerifest Dallas

*(third from top)*
Design Firm:
Michael Schwab
Studio
Art Director:
Louis Vargas
Designer:
Michael Schwab
Client:
Eddie Bauer

*(fourth from top)*
Design Firm:
Webster Design
Associates
Designer,
Illustrator:
Andrey Nagorny
Client:
Applied
Communications

*(bottom)*
Design Firm:
Pentagram Design
Art Director,
Designer:
Michael Bierut
Client:
Library of
Congress

SWIETERFEST

EDDIE BAUER
GLOBAL RELEAF
TREE PROJECT

PAVING THE WAY IN ACH

LIBRARY OF CONGRESS
BICENTENNIAL 1800·2000

*(this page)*
Design Firm:
Landor Associates
Creative Director:
Richard Brandt
Designer:
Craig Stout
Client: NYC2008

NYC2008

*(opposite)*
Design Firm:
Pennbaker.LMC
Creative Director:
Jeffrey McKay
Art Director,
Designer: Greg
Valdez
Client: Rathgeber/
Talley Wedding
Invitation

*(this page)*
Design Firm:
Sibley/Peteet
Design
Art Director,
Designer:
David Beck
Client:
Haggar
Clothing Co.

*(opposite, first from top)*
Design Firm:
Swieter Design
Art Director:
John Swieter
Designers:
John Swieter,
Mark Ford
Client:
Street Savage
Sportwear

*(second from top)*
Design Firm:
Michael Schwab
Studio
Creative Director:
Michael Schwab
Client:
Larry Mahan
Boots

*(third from top)*
Design Firm:
Mires Design,
Inc.
Art Director,
Designer:
José A. Serrano
Illustrator:
Tracy Sabin
Client: Chingones

*(bottom)*
Design Firm:
Charles S. Anderson
Design Co.
Art Director:
Charles S. Anderson
Designers:
Charles S. Anderson,
Paul Howalt,
Todd Piper-
Hauswirth
Client:
Sierra Designs

LOONEY TUNES
WB
COLLECTION
LOONEY TUNES
WB

von Gessl
stuffit

LOONEY TUNES
WB

van Gessl
S
Stuffit

*(this page)*
Design Firm:
Phoenix
Creative
Creative Director:
Eric Thoelke
Art Director,
Designer:
Kathy
Wilkinson
Client:
Venture Stores

*(opposite, top, bottom)*
Design Firm:
Sandstrom
Design
Art Director,
Designer: Steve
Sandstrom
Client:
Levi Strauss & Co.

*(opposite, middle)*
Design Firm:
Foote, Cone,
& Belding
Creative Director:
Brian Collius
Art Director,
Designer,
Photographer:
Joel Templin
Client:
Levi Strauss & Co.

Chums
USA

*(opposite)*
Design Firm:
Duffy Design
Client:
Chums Ltd.

*(this page)*
Design Firm:
Nike, Inc.
Creative Director:
Ron Dumas
Art Director,
Designer:
Webb Blevins
Illustrators:
Webb Blevins,
Michael
Phenning
Client: Nike

*(this page)*
Design Firm: Mires Design Inc.
Art Director: Jose A. Serrano
Designers: Deborah Horn, Jose A. Serrano
Illustrator: Tracy Sabin
Client: Industry Pictures

*(opposite, first from top)*
Design Firm: RBMM
Art Director, Designer, Illustrator: Jackson Wang
Client: Public Executions

*(second from top)*
Design Firm: Rigsby Design
Art Director: Lana Rigsby
Designers: Thomas Hull, Amy Wolpert
Illustrators: Andy Dearwater, David Bowman
Client: Gary Lankford

*(third from top)*
Design Firm: Mike Salisbury Communications
Art Director, Designer: Mike Salisbury
Illustrator: Mark Kawakami
Client: Michael Mann Productions

*(bottom)*
Design Firm: Signal Communications
Art Director, Designer, Illustrator: Scott Severson
Client: Picture Factory

ROLL'EM

*(this spread)*
Design Firm:
Cawrse & Effect
Art Director,
Designer,
Illustrator:
Andrew Cawrse
Client:
Cawrse & Effect

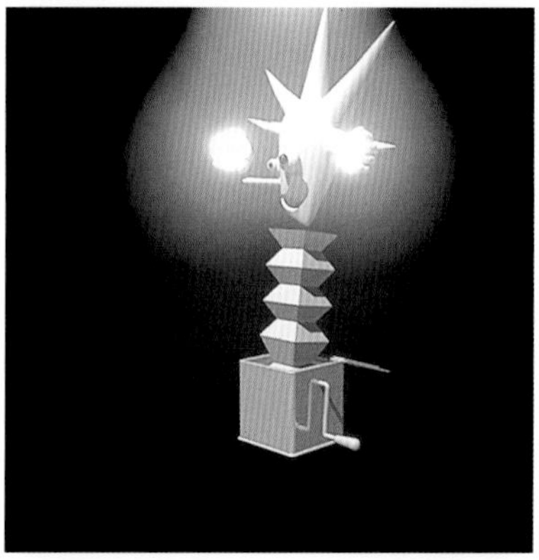

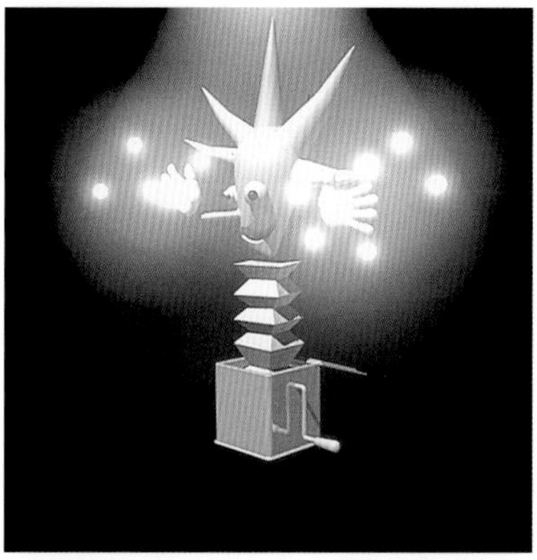

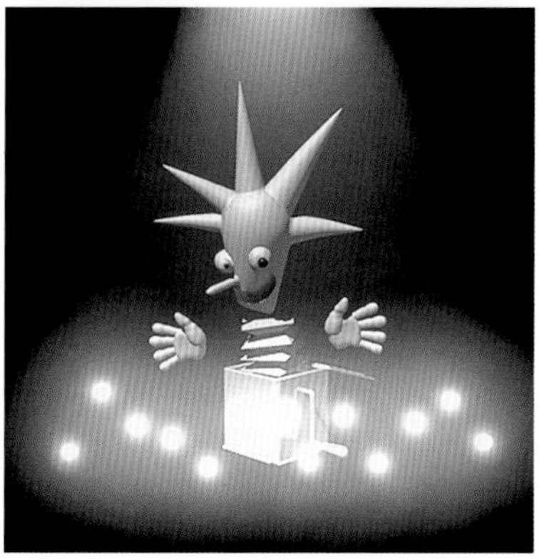

CAWRSE&EFFECT

*(this page)*
Design Firm:
Concrete Design
Communications
Inc.
Art Directors:
Diti Katona,
John Pylypczak
Designer,
Illustrator:
John Pylypczak
Client:
Stealing Time

*(opposite, top)*
Design Firm:
Brinkley Design
Designer,
Illustrator:
Corinne Lieney
Client:
Catwalk Digital

*(middle)*
Design Firm:
Primo Angeli,
Inc.
Creative Director:
Primo Angeli
Art Directors:
Carlo Pagoda,
Primo Angeli
Designers:
Marcelo
De Frietas,
Primo Angeli
Client:
San Francisco
Film Society

*(bottom)*
Design Firm:
Studio Rayolux
Designer:
Thad Boss
Client:
Blind Monkey
Productions

SAN FRANCISCO
INTERNATIONAL
FILM FESTIVAL

*(opposite, first from top)*
Design Firm: Brainstorm, Inc.
Art Director, Designer, Illustrator: Chuck Johnson
Client: Legacy Capital Group

*(second from top)*
Design Firm: Hornall Anderson Design Works, Inc.
Art Director: Jack Anderson
Designers: Jack Anderson, Debra Hampton, David Bates, Lisa Cerveny
Illustrator: John Fretz
Client: Stewart Capital Management

*(third from top)*
Design Firm: Brainstorm, Inc.
Art Director, Designer, Illustrator: Chuck Johnson
Client: Life Benefactors L.P.

*(fourth from top)*
Design Firm: KROG
Art Director, Designer: Edi Berk
Client: Slovenska Razvojna Druzba

*(bottom)*
Design Firm: The Office of Ted Fabella
Art Director, Designer: Ted Fabella
Client: Georgia Federal Bank

*(this page)*
Design Firm: Pollard Design
Designer, Illustrator: Jeff Pollard
Client: Grove Investment

*(this page)*
Design Firm:
Gonzolo Berro
Client:
Secretaria
de Deportes

*(opposite, first from top)*
Design Firm:
Gill Fishman
Assoicates
Creative Director,
Art Director:
Gill Fishman
Designer:
Tammy Torrey
Client: Combined
Jewish
Philanthropies

*(second from top)*
Design Firm:
Revolution Inc.
Creative Director:
John Phillips
Art Directors,
Designers: Jefferson
Wilkerson,
Jonathan Knecht
Client: Power &
Light District

*(third from top)*
Design Firm:
Shook Design
Group, Inc.
Art Director:
Ginger Riley
Designer:
Jeffrey Camillo
Client: Town of
Cornelius

*(fourth from top)*
Design Firm:
Reed & Steven
Client: Chamber
of Commerce,
Unlimited
Partnership
Division

*(bottom)*
Design Firm:
Brad Thomas
Graphic Design
Designer:
Brad Thompson
Client: Neighbors
for Neighborhoods

*(opposite, first from top)*
Design Firm: Peterson & Company
Client: Child Guidance

*(second from top)*
Design Firm: Slaughter Hanson
Designer: Marion English
Client: Optomology and Orthodontic's Clinic

*(third from top)*
Design Firm: Muller & Company
Creative Director: Susan Wilson
Art Director, Designer, Illustrator: Jeff Miller
Client: Center for Assistive Technology

*(fourth from top)*
Design Firm: Spangler Assoiciates, Inc.
Designer: Michael Connors
Client: Group HealthCooperative

*(bottom)*
Design Firm: Julie Johnson Design
Designer: Julie Johnson
Client: Mclean Prenatal Clinic

*(this page)*
Design Firm: Muller & Company
Creative Director: John Muller
Designer, Illustrator: Dave Swearingen
Client: Tazwell Hospital

*(this page)*
Design Firm:
Rickabaugh
Graphics
Art Directors:
Eric Rickabaugh,
Mark Krumel
Designer:
Michael Smith
Client:
Grant Medical
Center

*(opposite, top)*
Design Firm:
Antista Fairclough
Design
Art Director,
Designer:
Tom Antista
Client: National
Physician's
Network

*(middle)*
Design Firm:
S.D. Zyne
Designer:
Spencer Walters
Client:
The Art of
Dentistry

*(bottom)*
Design Firm:
Simple Green
Design
Creative Director:
Mike Brower
Designers:
Mike Brower,
Russ Acol-Scott
Client:
Department
of Power
(Spin Studio)

the ART of dentistry

The Park

*(opposite, first from top)*
Design Firm: Sibley/Peteet Design
Creative Director: Rex Peteet
Designer: Mark Brinkman
Client: Center for Marine Conservation

*(second from top)*
Design Firm: Farnet Hart Design Studio
Designers: Winnie Hart, T. J. Todd
Client: Audobon Exploration

*(third from top)*
Design Firm: Sommese Design
Creative Director, Illustrator: Lanny Sommese
Art Director, Designer: Kristin Breslin Sommese
Client: The Park Committee

*(fourth from top)*
Design Firm: Gardner Design
Creative Director: Brian Miller
Client: Kansas State University

*(bottom)*
Design Firm: Peterson & Company
Client: Women National Book Association

*(this page)*
Design Firm: A. Studio & Associates Co. Ltd.
Designer: Patrick Tam, Kwok Kee
Client: Lingnan Old Boy Association

*(this page)*
Design Firm:
Nagorny Design
Designer:
Andrey Nargorny
Client: Art Design
Guild

*(opposite, first from top)*
Design Firm:
Hixo Design
Designer: Tom Poth
Client: Corridor
Council

*(second from top)*
Design Firm:
RBMM
Art Director:
Jackson Wang
Client:
United Christian
Congregation

*(third from top)*
Design Firm:
Saatchi & Saatchi
Creative Director:
Dragan Sakan
Art Director,
Designer:
Slavimir Stojanovic
Client: XL Club
Discoteque

*(fourth from top)*
Design Firm:
Sullivan Perkins
Creative Director,
Designer:
Brett Barison
Client: Dallas
Public Library

*(bottom)*
Design Firm:
Wages Design
Creative Director:
Bob Wages
Designer:
Ted Fabella
Client: The
American Craft
Council

*(this page)*
Design Firm:
Bülent Erkmen
Designer:
Bülent Erkmen
Client: Friends
of Cuisine
Association

*(opposite, first from top)*
Design Firm:
RBMM/ The
Richards Group
Designer:
Horacio Cobos
Client: Multiple
Sclerosis Society

*(second from top)*
Design Firm:
Runyan Hinsche
Association
Art Director:
Jim Berte
Designer:
Jim Huerard
Client: Bancentro

*(third from top)*
Design Firm:
Michael Doret
Design
Creative Director,
Designer:
Michael Doret
Client: Graphic
Artists Guild

*(fourth from top)*
Designer: Marcus
Heinbach
Client:
Historische
Bauerschaft
Bleche

*(bottom)*
Design Firm:
Mike Salisbury
Communications
Creative Director:
Mike Salisbury
Client:
Power House

*(this page)*
Design Firm:
601 Design,Inc.
Creative Director:
Bruce Holdeman
Client: Rocky
Mountain Ostrich
Association

ROCKY MOUNTAIN
OSTRICH
ASSOCIATION

*(opposite)*
Design Firm:
Robertson Design
Art Directors:
John Robertson,
Jeff Carroll
Client: Heritage
Foundation

*(this page, first from top)*
Design Firm: Tracy Sabin Design
Art Director: Rita Hoffman
Illustrator: Tracy Sabin
Client: Taylor Guitars

*(second from top)*
Design Firm: Mires Design
Creative Director: José Serrano
Designers: José Serrano, Miguel Perez
Illustrator: Nancy Stahl
Client: Deleo Clay Tile

*(third from top)*
Design Firm: 601 Design Inc.
Creative Director, Designer: Bruce Holdeman
Client: Colorado Investment Casting

*(fourth from top)*
Design Firm: Mires Design
Creative Director, Designer: José Serrano
Illustrator: Tracy Sabin
Client: Deleo Clay Tiles

*(bottom)*
Design Firm: IMA Press Publishers
Creative Director, Designer: Anya Naumova
Client: JSC Mill Combine #4

*(opposite)*
Design Firm: Emery Vincent Design
Creative Director: Garry Emery
Client: Sakata Food Industries

SAKATA

L U N A

T E X T I L E S

*(opposite, first from top)*
Design Firm: Charles S. Anderson
Art Director: Charles S. Anderson
Designer: Jason Schulte
Client: Henry Engine Company

*(second from top)*
Design Firm: Gibbs Baronet
Creative Director, Designer: Bronson Ma
Art Directors: Willie Baronet, Steve Gibbs
Client: CreateTech

*(third from top)*
Design Firm: Vanderbyl Design
Creative Director: Michael Vanderbyl
Client: Luna Textiles

*(bottom)*
Design Firm: Savas Cekic Tasarim Ltd.
Creative Director, Designer: Savas Cekic
Client: Adres Ahsap Urunueri

*(this page)*
Design Firm: Sibley/Peteet Design
Creative Director: Rex Peteet
Designer: Mark Brinkman
Client: Tips Iron & Steel

PANGAEA

KELTY

ENGENHARIA DE PRODUÇÃO FUNELARIA

MISSOURI RIVER RIFLE WORKS

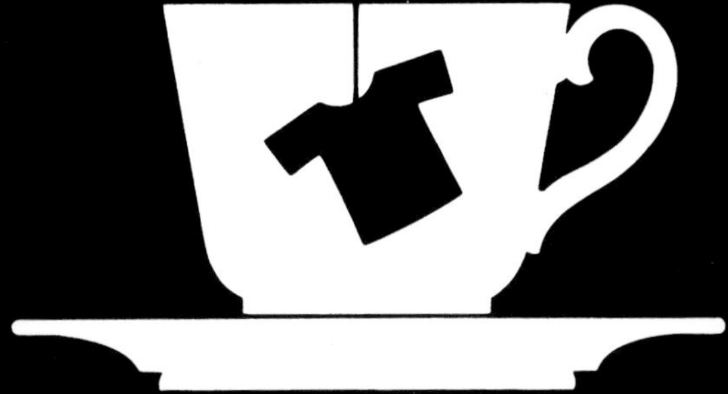

*(fourth from top)*
Design Firm:
Swieter Design U.S.
Creative Director,
Designer:
Mark Ford
Client:
Gestalt, Inc.

*(bottom)*
Design Firm:
Revolution, Inc.
Creative Director:
John Phillips
Art Director,
Designer:
Jefferson
Wilkinson
Client:
Missouri River

CARPENTER
Making your world comfortable.

*(opposite)*
Design Firm:
The Delor Group
Art Director:
Ken Delor
Designers:
Chris Enander,
Kevin Wyatt
Client:
Carpenter Co.

*(this page, first from top)*
Design Firm:
Graco
Advertising
Art Directors:
Schmidt, Parker,
and Dahl
Client:
Graco Contracter
Equipment
Division

*(second from top)*
Design Firm:
Art Force Studio
Art Director,
Designer:
Almassu Csaba
Client:
Lupus Vacuum
Ltd.

*(third from top)*
Design Firm:
Carlson
Marketing Group
Creative Director:
Stephan Färber
Client:
Lucent
Technologies

*(fourth from top)*
Design Firm:
Phoenix Creative
Art Director:
Ed Mantels-Seeker
Designers:
Ed Mantels-Seeker,
Luke Partridge
Client: St. Louis
Music/Flex Wave
Amplifiers

*(bottom)*
Design Firm:
RBMM
Art Director,
Designer:
Jackson Wang
Illustrator:
David Vaught
Client: Bear Creek
Woodworks

(nvolve)

PERSPECTA

AM CY

AMERICAN CYBERCAST

*(opposite, first from top)*
Design Firm: Pentagram Design
Art Director: Kit Hinrichs
Designer: Eric Collom
Client: nvolve, inc.

*(second from top)*
Design Firm: Sibley/Peteet Design
Art Director, Designer: Tom Kirsch
Client: Sibley/Peteet Design

*(third from top)*
Design Firm: Elixir Design
Art Director: Jennifer Jerde
Designer: Nate Durrant
Client: Perspecta, Inc.

*(fourth from top)*
Design Firm: Nesnadny + Schwartz
Creative Director, Designer: Gregory Oznowich
Client: Global Serve Corporation

*(bottom)*
Design Firm: CBO Multimedia Division
Art Director, Designer: Jill Taffet
Illustrator: Larry Wilcox
Client: American Cybercast

*(this page)*
Design Firm: St. John & Partners
Creative Director: Bruce Broder
Art Director, Designer: Jeff Rall
Client: Compuserve

*(this page)*
Design Firm: Swieter Design U.S.
Creative Director, Designer: Mark Ford
Client: Verve Creative

*(opposite, first from top)*
Design Firm: Drive Communications
Creative Director, Designer: Michael Graziolo
Client: Vuepoint

*(second from top)*
Design Firm: Thom & Dave Marketing Design
Client: Vision X

*(third from top)*
Design Firm: Mires Design Inc.
Creative Director: John Ball
Designers: John Ball, Miguel Perez
Client: McGraw Hill

*(fourth from top)*
Design Firm: Cawrse and Effect
Creative Director, Designer: Andrew Cawrse
Client: Originalis Custom Programming

*(bottom)*
Design Firm: Swieter Design U.S.
Creative Director, Designer: Mark Ford
Client: Saturn Interactive Media

VISION X
SOFTWARE INC

HOME INTERACTIVE
McGraw-Hill

ORIGINALIS

*(this page)*
Design Firm: Cawrse & Effect
Creative Director, Designer: Andrew Cawrse
Client: BB Interactive

*(opposite, first from top)*
Design Firm: Authaus
Art Director: Clint Gorthy
Client: W3 Productions

BB-INTERACTIVE

*(second from top)*
Design Firm: Mires Design
Creative Director: John Ball
Designers: John Ball, Deborah Horn
Client: Fusion Media

*(third from top)*
Design Firm: Viscom Design Group
Art Director: Mark Wood
Designer: Sara Walters
Client: Visual Matter

*(bottom)*
Design Firm: Studio Archetype
Creative Director, Designer: Andrew Cawrse
Client: Nintendo of America Inc.

FUSION MEDIA

VISUAL MATTER

BLAST CORPS

*(this page, first, third, bottom from top)*
Design Firm: Maddocks+Co.
Art Directors: Tika Buchanan, Julia Precht
Designer, Illustrator: Tika Buchanan
Client: American Craft Museum

A CELEBRATION OF THE AMERICAN TABLE
THE BANQUET

SFMOMA
SAN FRANCISCO MUSEUM OF MODERN ART

A CELEBRATION OF THE AMERICAN TABLE
THE BANQUET

*(second from top)*
Design Firm: Michael Osborne Design
Art Director: Michael Osborne
Client: San Francisco Modern Museum of Art

*(opposite)*
Design Firm: Carre Noir
Art Director, Designer: Michel Disle
Photographer: Oliver Girard
Client: Miho Museum

A CELEBRATION OF THE AMERICAN TABLE
THE BANQUET

MIHO
MUSEUM

Museum of Science

*(opposite)*
Design Firm: Brandequity International
Art Director, Designer: Joseph Selame
Client: Museum of Science

*(this page, first from top)*
Design Firm: Deep Design
Art Director, Designer: Mark Steingruber
Illustrator: Chris Spollen
Client: U.S Space and Rocket Center

*(second from top)*
Design Firm: Nippon Design Center
Art Director, Designer: Nagai Kazumasa
Client:Chiba City Museum of Art

*(third from top)*
Design Firm: Authaus
Art Director, Designer: Clint Gorthy
Client: Pearson Air Museum

*(fourth from top)*
Design Firm: Pentagram Design
Art Director, Designer: Justus Oehler
Client: Musuem Für Post Und Kommunication

*(bottom)*
Design Firm: Mires Design
Art Director: John Ball
Designers: John Ball, Gale Spitzley
Client: California Center for the Arts

GOLDEN
APPLES

Santa Cruz
Surfing museum

SALT LAKE ART CENTER

ROYAL ARMOURIES MUSEUM

*(opposite, first from top)*
Design Firm: GSD&M Advertising
Designer: Brett Stiles
Client: Golden Apples

*(second from top)*
Design Firm: Labbé Design Co.
Art Director, Designer: Jeff Labbé
Client: Santa Cruz Surf Museum

*(third from top)*
Design Firm: New Mexico Studio of Design
Creative Director, Designer: Ronnie Garver
Art Director: Louis Ocepek
Illustrator: Michael Kiernan
Client: New Mexico State University Art Gallery

*(fourth from top)*
Design Firm: Arrowood Design
Art Director, Designer: Scott Arrowood
Client: Salt Lake Art Center

*(bottom)*
Design Firm: Minale Tattersfield
Client: Royal Armouries Museum

*(this page)*
Design Firm: Alternativ Studio
Art Director: Péter Vajda
Client: Centrális Galéria

*(this page)*
Design Firm:
Reed and
Steven
Art Directors:
Matt Cave,
Russel Parker
Designer:
Matt Cave
Client:
Bluxo Records

*(opposite, first from top)*
Design Firm:
Studio
Rayolux
Designer:
Thad Boss
Client:
Tensonic
Records

*(second from top)*
Design Firm:
Widgets &
Stone
Designer:
Brian Woodlief
Client:
Jennifer Daniels

*(third from top)*
Design Firm: Zamboo
Designer:
Dave Zambotti
Client:
Baton Records

*(fourth from top)*
Design Firm:
Deep Design
Designer,
Illustrator: Rick
Grimsley
Client:
Cherokee
Mud

*(bottom)*
Design Firm: Brinkley
Design
Designer:
Leigh Brinkley
Illustrator:
Corrine Genevi
Client: Wyndham
Music

Taylor Guitars

Taylor Guitars

VOLCANO

Taylor Guitars

Taylor Guitars

Designer:
Miguel Perez
Illustrator:
Michael Schwab
Client:
Taylor Guitars

*(opposite, first from top)*
Art Directors: Jeri Heiden, Michael Rey
Designer: Greg Lindy
Client: Warner Bros. Records

*(second from top)*
Design Firm: Sullivan Hernadon
Creative Director: Mark Sullivan
Art Director, Designer, Illustrator: Kris Murphy
Client: Loomis Productions

# H

*(this page; opposite, middle)*
Design Firm: Packaging Create Inc.
Art Director: Akio Okumura
Designer: Emi Kajihara
Client: New Oji Paper Co., Ltd.

*(opposite, top, bottom)*
Design Firm: Mires Design, Inc.
Art Director: Jose A. Serrano
Designer: Jose A. Serrano, Miguel Perez
Illustrator: Tracy Sabin
Client: Greenfield Paper Company

GROW A NOTE
The Notecard You Plant
GREEN FIELD PAPER COMPANY

OJI PAPER GALLERY GINZA

HEMP HERITAGE

*(this page; opposite, third from top)*
Design Firm:
VSA Partners, Inc.
Creative Director:
Dana Arnett
Designer:
Jason Eplawy
Client:
Potlatch Corp.

*(opposite, first, fourth from top)*
Design Firm:
Charles S. Anderson
Design Company
Art Director:
Charles S. Anderson
Designer:
Jason Schulte
Client: French
PaperCompany

POTLATCH
McCOY™
THE PAPER ALL OTHERS
ARE JUDGED BY

*(second from top)*
Design Firm: Hambly
& Woolley Inc.
Client: Hambly
& Woolley
Papergoods

*(bottom)*
Design Firm:
Pentagram Design
Art Directors:
Woody Pirtle,
John Klotnia
Designers:
John Klotnia,
Ivette Montee
de Oca
Client: Champion
International Corp.

french 125 paper

Hambly & Woolley
PaperGoods

A CENTURY OF PAPERMAKING
1898 100 1998
POTLATCH

F P C

METER

*(opposite, first from top)*
Design Firm: Rovillo Design Associates
Art Director: Chris Rovillo
Designer, Illustrator: Sarah Moriarty
Client: Ray Hand Photography

*(second from top)*
Design Firm: Templin Design
Art Director, Designer, Illustrator: Joel Templin
Client: Jon Gipe Photo

*(third from top)*
Design Firm: Sibley/Peteet Design
Art Director, Designer: Tom Kirsch
Client: King Photography

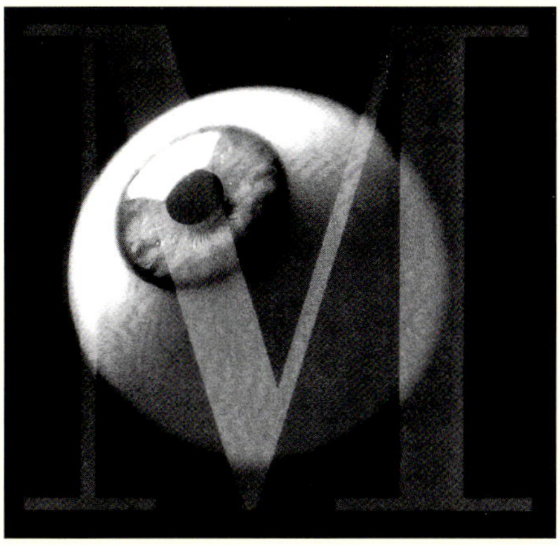

*(bottom)*
Design Firm: Weiss, Whitten, Stagliano
Client: Meter

*(this page)*
Design Firm: Signall Communications
Art Director, Designer: Scott Severson
Illustrator: Dan Mullen
Client: Dan Mullen Photography

*(this page)*
Design Firm:
Felix Sockwell
Creative
Art Director,
Designer:
Felix Sockwell
Client:
Carol Kaelson

*(opposite, first from top)*
Design Firm:
Mires Design
Art Director,
Designer:
José Serrano
Client: Antonio
Mercado

*(second from top)*
Design Firm:
Storm Design
& Advertising
Creative Director,
Designer:
Dean Butler,
David Ansett
Client: Paul West
Photography

*(third from top)*
Design Firm:
Muller &
Company
Art Director,
Designer,
Illustrator:
John Muller
Client: Michael
Regnier
Photography

*(bottom)*
Design Firm:
Signal
Communications
Art Director,
Designer:
Scott Severson
Client: Bruce
Wagman
Photography

PHOTOGRAPHY
1242 BARFORD AVE.
HACIENDA HEIGHTS
CALIFORNIA 91745
TEL (818) 333-7754
ANTONIO MERCADO

PAUL WEST
PHOTOGRAPHY

BRUCE WAGMAN
PHOTOGRAPHY

*(this page)*
Design Firm: Vanderbyl Design
Creative Director, Art Director: Michael Vanderbyl
Client: The American Center for Wine, Food and the Arts

*(opposite)*
Design Firm: Drive Communications
Art Director, Designer: Michael Graziolo
Client: BMW Zentrum

Pantone 158

Pantone 200

Pantone 299

Pantone 3415

Pantone 526

Pantone 661

Pantone 158

*(this page)*
Design Firm:
Principa Graphica
Art Directors:
Robin Rickabaugh,
Heidi Rickabaugh
Designer:
Clint Gorthy
Client:
Dynagraphics

*(opposite, first from top)*
Design Firm:
Insight Design
Communications
Art Directors,
Designers:
Sherrie Holdeman,
Tracy Holdeman
Client: Prairie Print

*(second from top)*
Design Firm:
Tracy Sabin
Graphic Design
Art Director:
Jim Gordon
Illustrator:
Tracy Sabin
Client: Gordon
Screen Printing

*(third from top)*
Design Firm:
Greteman Group
Creative Director,
Art Director:
Sonia Greteman
Designers:
Sonia Greteman,
James Strange
Client: LePrint
Express

*(fourth from top)*
Designer:
Leo Kopelow
Client: CSE Inc.

*(bottom)*
Design Firm:
Savas Cekic
Tasarim Ltd.
Creative Director,
Art Director,
Designer: Savas Cekic
Client: Surmeli
Grafik

*(this page)*
Design Firm:
Butler Kemp Design,
Art Director, Designer:
Butler Kemp Design
Client: Southweb Printing

*(opposite, first from top)*
Design Firm:
Hixo Inc.
Art Director, Designer:
Mike Hicks
Client: Inkspots

*(second from top)*
Design Firm:
Porkka Visual KY
Designer:
Antti Porkka
Client: Nykypaind Oy

SOUTHWEB PRINTING

*(third from top)*
Design Firm:
DBD International
Creative Director, Art Director, Designer:
David Brier
Client: West Wind Graphics

*(fourth from top)*
Design Firm:
Mires Design
Art Director:
José Serrano
Designers:
José Serrano, Miguel Perez
Client: Bordeaux Printers

*(bottom)*
Design Firm:
Elixir Design
Art Director:
Jennifer Jerde
Designer:
Michael Braley
Client: Premier

*(this page, first from top)*
Design Firm: Mires Design Inc.
Client: Terra Sketch

*(second from top)*
Design Firm: Lewis Advertising/Nashville
Creative Director: Cindy Sargent
Art Director: Robert Froedge
Client: Neogenesis

*(third from top)*
Design Firm: Ross Patrick/Los Angeles
Art Director, Designer, Illustrator: Ross Patrick
Client: Broadleaf Cigars

*(fourth from top)*
Design Firm: Sayles Graphic Design
Art Director, Designer, Illustrator: John Sayles
Client: Christine's 20th Century

*(bottom)*
Design Firm: RBMM
Creative Director, Art Director, Designer: Shayne Washburn
Client: InfaCare

*(opposite)*
Design Firm: Addis Group
Art Director: David Leong
Designers: David Leong, Paul Dorian, Justin Oberbauer
Illustrators: Robin Maclean, Trevor Wright (Hamagami-Carroll & Assoc.)
Client: Solaris Group

# FIRE ANT KILLER

*(this page, first from top)*
Design Firm: Graphic Solutions Inc.
Creative Director: Marc Tebon
Designer: Mike Magestro
Client: The Paintsmith

*(second from top)*
Design Firm: Mires Design
Art Director: José A. Serrano
Designers: José A. Serrano, Miguel Perez
Client: All Pro Wallpaper

*(third from top)*
Design Firm: Savas Cekic Tasarim Ltd.
Creative Director, Art Director, Designer: Savas Cekic
Client: Ova Insan Kaynakliar-Detachering

*(bottom)*
Design Firm: Zoom
Art Director, Designer: Priit Isok
Client: Fortuuna Loto Ltd.

*(opposite, top)*
Design Firm: Felix Sockwell Design
Client: Kaelson Co. Integrated Landscapes

*(middle)*
Creative Director, Designer: Ruth Bielobocky
Client: David Bielobocky

*(bottom)*
Design Firm: Mullen Advertising
Creative Director: Art Director, Designer: Ginger Hood
Photographer: Hans Neleman
Client: Osram Sylvania

ALL-PRO
WALLPAPERING
INSTALLATION
AND REMOVAL

SYLVANIA
IDEAS THAT BUILD BUSINESS

*(this page)*
Design Firm:
Fuszion Art & Design
Creative Director, Art Director:
Anthony Fletcher
Designers:
Anthony Fletcher, Richard Lee Heffner
Client: Wordsworth

*(opposite, first from top)*
Design Firm:
Sibley/Peteet Design
Creative Director, Designer:
Rex Peteet
Client:
Performing Pets

*(second from top)*
Design Firm:
Hornall Anderson Design Works
Creative Director, Art Director:
Jack Anderson
Designers:
Jack Anderson, Debra McCloskey, David Bates, Lisa Cerveny
Illustrator: John Fretz
Client: Stewart Capital Management

*(third from top)*
Design Firm:
Lippa Pearce Design
Creative Directors:
Harry Pearce, Dimenil Lippa
Designer:
Harry Pearce
Client:
Richard Foster

*(fourth from top)*
Design Firm:
PPA Design Ltd.
Art Director, Designer:
Byron Jacobs
Client: Valuation Services Ltd.

*(bottom)*
Design Firm:
Pennebaker.LMC
Creative Director:
Jeffrey McKay
Art Director, Designer:
David Lerch
Client: Odyssey Marine Shipping Inc.

AquaPenn
spring water company
Visitors
Shipping
Receiving

*(opposite)*
Design Firm:
Sommese Design
Art Directors:
Kristin Breslin
Sommese,
Lanny Sommese
Photographer:
Paul Hazi
Designer:
Amy Zuckerman
Client:
Aqua Penn Spring
Water Company

*(this page,*
*first from top)*
Design Firm:
Labbé Design Co.
Creative Director,
Designer:
Jeff Labbé
Photographer:
Kimball Hall
Illustrator:
CSA Archives
Client: The Tech
Factory

*(second from top)*
Design Firm:
Curtis Design
Creative Director:
David Curtis
Designer:
Sean McGrath
Client:
World Wide
Welding Inc.

*(third from top)*
Design Firm:
Mires Design
Client: Jennifer
Sands

*(fourth from top)*
Design Firm:
Art Force Studio
Art Director,
Designer, Illustrator:
Alma'ssy Csaba
Client:
Business Power
System Ltd.

*(bottom)*
Design Firm:
Arrowood Design
Creative Director,
Designer, Illustrator:
Scott Arrowood
Client:
Envoy Staffing

PAPER
PAPER
MAGAZINE
PAPER
PAPER
PAPER
PAPER
PAPER
PAPER
PAPER
PAPER
PAPER
PAPER

*(this page)*
Design Firm:
Mires Design Inc.
Creative Director,
Art Director:
Scott Mires
Designer:
Deborah Hom
Illustrator:
Tracy Sabin
Client: Harcourt
Brace & Co.

*(opposite, first from top)*
Design Firm:
Principia Graphica
Art Directors:
Robin Rickabaugh,
Heidi Rickabaugh
Designer:
Clint Gorthy
Client: Starbound
Publishing

*(second from top)*
Design Firm:
Franke
Communications
Art Director,
Designer:
Carsten Franke
Client:
Maas & Hollweg

*(third from top)*
Design Firm:
Mires Design
Art Director,
Designer:
Scott Mires
Illustrator:
Tracy Sabin
Client: Harcourt
Brace & Co.

*(fourth from top)*
Design Firm:
Robertson Design
Art Directors:
John Robertson,
Jeff Carroll
Designer:
Jeff Carroll
Client:
Discipleship
Resources

*(bottom)*
Design Firm:
Ephemera, Inc.
Creative Director:
Joseph Montebello
Designer:
Greg Simpson
Client:
HarperCollins

PASSPORTS

HARPER FLAMINGO

*(this page)*
Design Firm: Michael Brock Design
Creative Director, Designer: Michel Brock
Client: Regent Properties

*(opposite, first from top)*
Design Firm: Mires Design
Art Director, Designer: José Serrano
Illustrator: Dan Thoner
Client: Davidson Communities

*(second from top)*
Design Firm: Pentagram Design
Art Director: Michael Bierut
Designers: Michael Bierut, Dorit Lev
Client: Gotham Equities

REGENT PROPERTIES

*(third from top)*
Design Firm: Rovillo Design Associates
Creative Director: Chris Rovillo
Designers: Chris Rovillo, Marian Moore, Tammy Yarugadda
Client: Urban Home

*(fourth from top)*
Design Firm: Eisenberg & Associates
Creative Director: Saul Torres
Art Director, Designer: Larry White
Client: Eisenberg Skatepark

*(bottom)*
Design Firm: RBMM
Art Director, Designer, Illustrator: Jackson Wang
Client: Cop Ranch/ Ashley Cop

TESORO
TUSCANY HILLS

URBAN
HOME

CHAOS
LURES

URZA'S
SAGA

SKY'S
THE LIMIT

*(opposite, first from top)*
Design Firm: Mires Design
Art Director, Designer: Jose Serrano
Illustrator: Tracy Sabin
Client: Chaos

*(second from top)*
Design Firm: Vanderbyl Design
Client: Windquest (DeVos Family)

*(third from top)*
Design Firm: Wizards of the Coast
Creative Director: Chaz Elliot
Art Director, Designer: Daniel Gelon

*(fourth from top)*
Design Firm: Point Zero
Client: Oak Valley Golf Course

*(bottom)*
Design Firm: Antista Fairclough Design
Client: Sky's The Limit

*(this page)*
Design Firm: Wizards of the Coast
Creative Director: Rich Kaalaas
Art Director: Dana Kuurtson
Designer: Dana Kuurtson & Corey Macourek
Client: Jim Lee's C-23

*(this page)*
Design Firm:
RBMM
Creative Director,
Designer:
Shayne
Washburn
Client:
Austin Gym

*(opposite, first from top)*
Design Firm:
Mires Design
Art Director,
Designer:
José Serrano
Illustrator:
Dan Thoner
Client:
San Diego
Hiking Club

*(second from top)*
Design Firm:
Felix Sockwell
Creative
Designer:
Felix Sockwell
Client:
Shimano

*(third from top)*
Design Firm:
CKS NY
Creative Director:
Jill Savini
Art Director:
John Connelly
Client:
Vail Resorts
Inc.

*(bottom)*
Design Firm:
Fielhauer Menken
Tomaszewski
Creative Director:
Jakob Fielhauer
Designer:
Brett Kastenholz
Client:
S&L Farms

*(this page)*
Design Firm:
Nike Inc.
(in house)
Art Directors:
Jason Bacon,
Greg Hoffman
Illustrator:
Jason Bacon
Client: Nike Inc.

*(opposite, first from top)*
Design Firm:
Michael
Stanard Design
Art Directors:
Michael Stanard,
Marc Fuhrman
Designer:
Mark Fuhrman
Client: Lionel

*(second from top)*
Design Firm:
601 Design Inc.
Creative Director,
Designer, Illustrator:
Bruce Holdeman
Client: The
Denver Post

*(third from top)*
Design Firm:
Mires Design Inc.
Creative Director,
Designer:
José A. Serrano
Illustrator:
Tracy Sabin
Client: Boy Scout
Troop 260

*(fourth from top)*
Design Firm:
Hornall Anderson
Design Works
Art Director:
Jack Anderson
Designers:
Jack Anderson,
Nicole Bloss
Client: Tom
Stewart "M"

*(bottom)*
Design Firm:
The Flowers Group
Art Director:
Cory Sheehan
Illustrator:
Tracy Sabin
Client: The Ridge
Resort

*(this page)*
Design Firm:
Pentagram Design, Inc.
Art Director:
Paula Scher
Designer:
Michael Beirut
Client:
The Fashion Center

*(opposite, first from top)*
Design Firm:
Nike, Inc. (in-house)
Client:
Niketown

**THE FASHION CENTER**

*(second from top)*
Design Firm:
Michael Doret Graphic Design
Art Director, Designer, Illustrator:
Michael Doret
Client:
Chic-A-Boom

*(third from top)*
Design Firm:
Mark Oliver, Inc.
Art Director, Designer, Illustrator:
Mark Oliver
Client:
Breeder's Choice

*(bottom)*
Design Firm:
Mires Design, Inc.
Art Director, Designer:
José A. Serrano
Illustrator:
Dan Thoner
Client:
Hell Racer

harvest
*market*

harvest
*market*

harvest
*market*

harvest
*market*

Design Firm:
Jager di Paolo
Kemp Design
Client:
Harvest Market



harvest
market

PARK
MEADOWS

*(opposite)*
Design Firm: Communication Arts Inc.
Art Director: Henry Beer
Designer: Mike Doyle
Photographer: Aaron Hoffman
Client: Trizec Hahn

*(this page, first from top)*
Design Firm: Coy
Art Director: John Coy
Designers: John Coy, Albert Choi, Rokha Srey
Photographer: David J. Williams
Client: Pieces

*(second from top)*
Design Firm: Hornall Anderson Design Works
Art Director: Jack Anderson
Designers: Jack Anderson, Larry Anderson, Julie Keenan
Client: Xcel

*(third from top)*
Design Firm: Arias Associates
Art Director: Mauricio Arias
Designers: Mauricio Arias, Vahn Phan, Steve Mortensen
Illustrator: Harry Bates
Client: Francesca Freedman

*(fourth from top)*
Design Firm: Hornall Anderson Design Works
Art Director: Jack Anderson
Designers: Jack Anderson, Larry Anderson, Julie Keena
Illustrator: Dave Julian
Client: Alta Beverage Company

*(bottom)*
Design Firm: Michael Schwab Studio
Art Directors: Dave Straus, George Szakall
Designer, Illustrator: Michael Schwab
Client: Sloat Garden Center

*(this page, first from top)*
Design Firm:
Royal Rocket Studio
Art Director, Designer, Illustrator:
Halasi Zolta'n
Client:
Taljebbini Kereskedelmi KFT

*(second from top)*
Design Firm:
Hornall Anderson Design Works
Art Director:
Jack Anderson
Designers:
Jack Anderson, Jana Nishi
Client:
Seattle Chocolate Company

*(third from top)*
Design Firm:
Gerstman & Meyers Inc.
Creative Director:
Juan Concepcion
Designer:
Susan Payne
Client:
Hannaford Brothers Co.

*(fourth from top)*
Design Firm:
Martin Design
Designer:
David Martin
Client:
Sporting Footgear

*(bottom)*
Design Firm:
Mires Design
Art Director, Designer:
José A. Serrano
Illustrator:
Dan Thoner
Client:
Adventure 16

*(opposite)*
Design Firm:
Pentagram Design
Art Director:
Kit Hinrichs
Designer:
Jackie Foshaug
Client:
The Gymboree Corporation

GYMBOREE

*(this page, top)*
Design Firm:
Graphic Design Solutions
Designer:
Angie Dudley
Client:
Atlanta Humane Society

*(middle)*
Design Firm:
Mires Design
Art Director:
José A. Serrano
Designers:
José A. Serrano, Mark Mattingly
Client:
Ocotillo Rocket Club

*(bottom)*
Design Firm:
Carrmichael Design
Designer:
Michael Carr
Client:
Herb Rosen/ Liar's Club

*(opposite, top)*
Design Firm:
Z.3 Design
Art Director, Designer:
Gary Williams
Client:
Alan Bogdanoff Surfboards

*(middle)*
Design Firm:
Nike Image Design
Designer:
Derek Welch
Client:
Nike Ltd.

*(bottom)*
Design Firm:
Duffy Design
Creative Director:
Joe Duffy
Art Director:
Neil Powell
Designers, Illustrators: Neil Powell, Alan Leusink
Client: Hart Ski

Social 214,215

*(this page, first from top)*
Design Firm:
Swieter Design
U.S.
Creative Director:
John Swieter
Designer:
Cameron Smith
Client:
DDB
Needham

*(second from top)*
Design Firm:
Ross Patrick
Los Angeles
Art Director,
Designer,
Illustrator:
Ross Patrick
Client:
Kybartas Fitness

*(third from top)*
Design Firm:
Tinguely Concept
SA
Designer:
Johann Terrettaz
Client:
Nidecker
Snowboard Factory

*(fourth from top)*
Design Firm:
Simple Green
Design
Art Director,
Designer:
Mike Brower
Client:
Bod.E Precision

*(bottom)*
Design Firm:
Mires Design Inc.
Art Director:
José A. Serrano
Designers:
José A. Serrano,
Furniko Tamura
Illustrator:
Furniko Tamura
Client:
San Diego
Cycling Club

*(opposite)*
Design Firm:
Baden Design
Art Director,
Designer:
Sahron Baden
Photographer:
Felixco
Client: Team
Bayside

TEAM BAYSIDE TEAM BAYSIDE

*(this page)*
Design Firm:
Mires Design Inc.
Art Director:
John Ball
Designers:
John Ball,
Miguel Perez
Illustrator:
Tracy Sabin
Client: Nike Inc.

*(opposite)*
Design Firm:
Nike Design
Art Director,
Designer:
Jeff Weithman
Client: Nike, Inc.

*(this page)*
Design Firm:
Designworks
Creative Director:
Nigel Swinn
Designer:
Bill Carden Horton
Client: TAB

*(opposite)*
Design Firm:
Malcolm Grear
Designers, Inc.
Art Director:
Malcolm Grear
Client: Atlanta
Committee for the
Olympic Games

TOUCH

EFX

BY CONVERSE®

™

REI

*(this page)*
Design Firm:
Pentagram
Design Ltd.
Creative Director:
Justus Oehler
Client:
Best People Ltd.

*(opposite, first from top)*
Design Firm:
VSA Partners
Art Directors:
Dana Arnett,
Melissa Waters
Designers:
Curtis Schreiber,
Ken Fox,
Adam Smith
Client: Harley-Davidson Inc.

Best.

*(second from top)*
Design Firm:
Smith, Ghormley,
Lofgreen Design
Client:
Trax Tech, Inc.

*(third from top)*
Design Firm:
Sullivan Perkins
Designer:
Kelly Allen
Client: The Rouse Company

*(bottom)*
Design Firm:
BNA Design
Limited
Creative Director,
Designer:
Diana Bidwill
Client:
W. Anchor Ltd.

*(this page, first from top)*
Design Firm: PPA Design Ltd.
Art Directors: Byron Jacobs, Joe Kurzer, Bethany Bunnell
Designer: Byron Jacobs
Client: STAR Radio

*(second from top)*
Design Firm: Essex Two
Creative Director, Designer: Joseph Michael Essex
Illustrator: John Knowles
Client: NEC Technologies

*(third from top)*
Design Firm: McMillan Design
Art Director, Designer: William McMillan
Client: KC Video

*(fourth from top)*
Design Firm: Button Design Company
Art Director, Designer: Dominic Carroll
Client: Meteor Video Services

*(bottom)*
Design Firm: Haley Johnson Design Co.
Art Director: Haley Johnson
Designer: Richard Boynton
Client: Matre Productions

*(opposite)*
Design Firm: Geer Design, Inc.
Art Director, Designer: Mark Geer
Client: Times 3 Productions

*(first from top)*
Design Firm:
Kirby Stephens
Design, Inc.
Art Directors:
Kirby Stephens,
Bill Jones
Designer:
Bill Jones
Client: Russell
County Tourist
Commission

*(second from top)*
Design Firm:
Art Force Studio
Designer:
Halasi Zoltan
Client:Hungarian
Academy of Crafts
and Design

*(third from top)*
Design Firm:
Mires Design, Inc.
Art Director,
Designer:
José A. Serrano
Illustrator:
Dan Thoner
Client:
Palm Springs

*(bottom)*
Design Firm:
Balance Design
Designer:
Scott Dvorak
Client:
Flying Colors

# Indices Verzeichnis Index

# Creative Directors Art Directors Designers

# Design Firms Agencies

# Clients

GRAPHIS
313

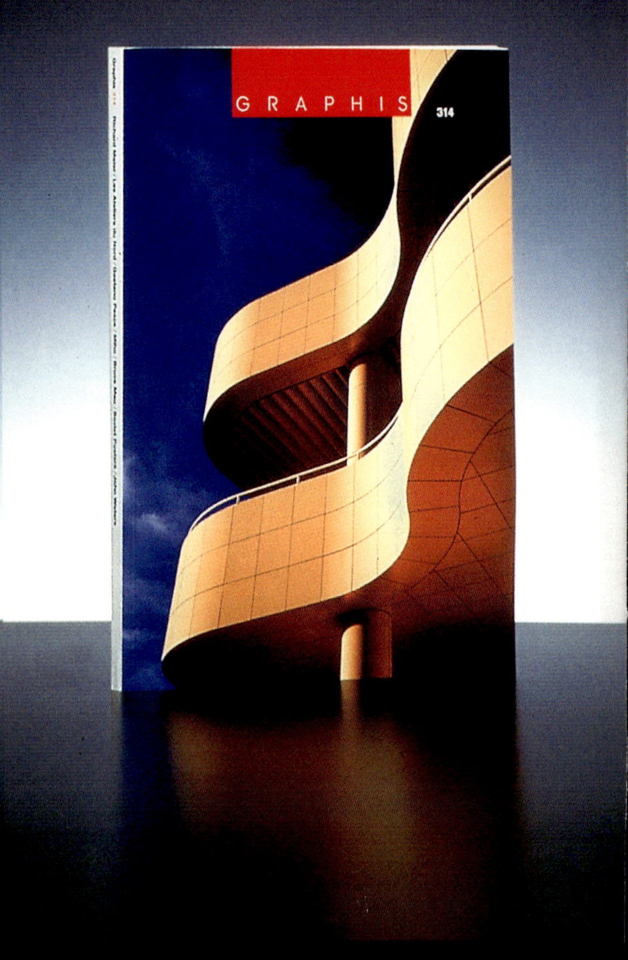
GRAPHIS
314

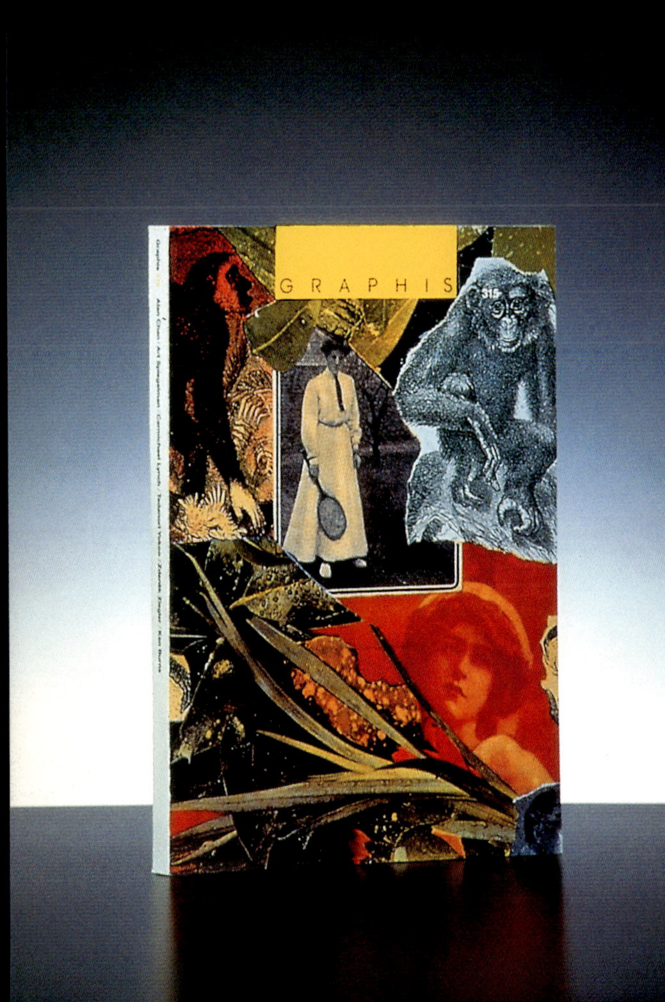
GRAPHIS

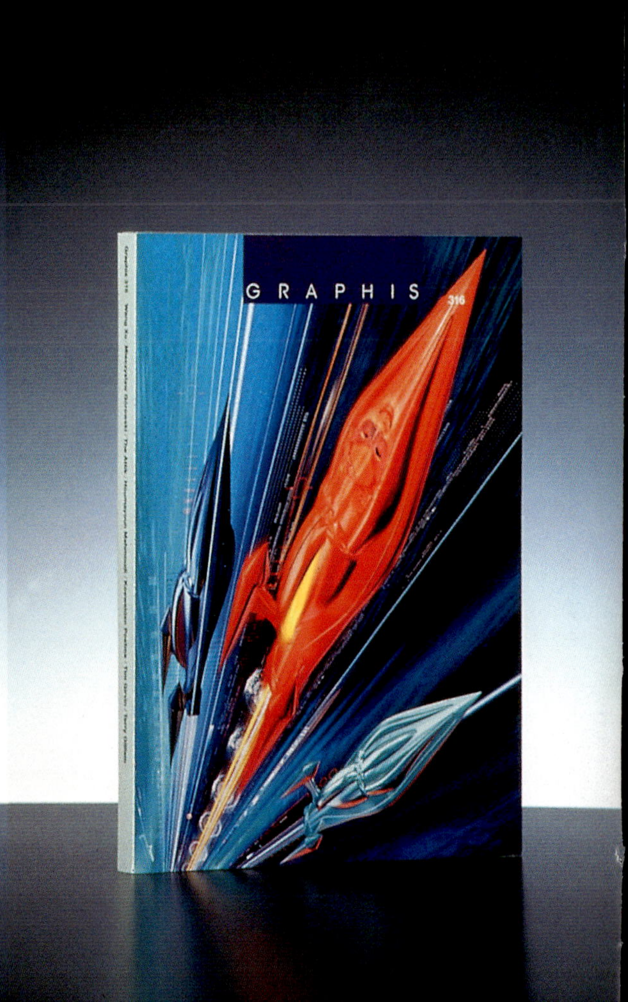
GRAPHIS
316

GRAPHIS
PosterAnnual1998
Corporate Identity 3
Book Design 2
New Talent Design Annual 1998
GRAPHIS PRODUCT DESIGN 2
PRODUCT DESIGN
T-shirtDesign2
BURY YOUR BONES
In Levi's
GRAPHIS DESIGN 98
DESIGN
BOTTLE DESIGN
GRAPHIS BOTTLE DESIGN
AppleDesign
AppleDesign The Work of the Apple Industrial Design Group

## Order Form

As a subscriber to the magazine, you automatically qualify for a *40 percent discount* on any of our books. If you place a standing order you will receive a *50 percent discount.* This means any Graphis book you select is sent to you as soon as it comes off press, and you will be billed at half the cover price plus shipping. With a *standing order* Graphis doesn't have to go through the expense of contacting you by mail and can therefore pass the savings directly back to you. Our annuals such as Poster, Photo, Design, and Advertising come out every year. The rest of our books come out every 2-4 years. If you don't wish to receive a particular book automatically when it happens to come out just choose the *40 percent off price.* If you are not a subscriber, then you still receive a *20 percent discount.* For your support we now cover all the communication disciplines and if there is a Graphis book you care to have that is not listed, please call us and we will do everything we can to get it for you. We thank you for your support.

| Book Title | Retail | Non Subscriber 20% off | Subscriber 40% off | Standing Order 50% off | Quantity | Totals |
|---|---|---|---|---|---|---|
| **Spring Books 1998** | | | | | | |
| **Book Design 2** | ☐ $70 | ☐ $56 | ☐ $42 | ☐ $35 | | |
| **Corporate Identity 3** | ☐ $70 | ☐ $56 | ☐ $42 | ☐ $35 | | |
| **New Talent 1998** | ☐ $60 | ☐ $48 | ☐ $36 | ☐ $30 | | |
| **Poster Annual 1998** | ☐ $70 | ☐ $56 | ☐ $42 | ☐ $35 | | |
| **T-Shirt 2** | ☐ $60 | ☐ $48 | ☐ $36 | ☐ $30 | | |
| **Fall Books 1998** | | | | | | |
| **Advertising 1999** | ☐ $70 | ☐ $56 | ☐ $42 | ☐ $35 | | |
| **Annual Reports 6** | ☐ $70 | ☐ $56 | ☐ $42 | ☐ $35 | | |
| **Brochures 3** | ☐ $70 | ☐ $56 | ☐ $42 | ☐ $35 | | |
| **Design Annual 1999** | ☐ $70 | ☐ $56 | ☐ $42 | ☐ $35 | | |
| **Digital Photo 1** | ☐ $70 | ☐ $56 | ☐ $42 | ☐ $35 | | |
| **Letterhead 4** | ☐ $70 | ☐ $56 | ☐ $42 | ☐ $35 | | |
| **Logo Design 4** | ☐ $60 | ☐ $48 | ☐ $36 | ☐ $30 | | |
| **Photo Annual 1998** | ☐ $70 | ☐ $56 | ☐ $42 | ☐ $35 | | |

| Book Title | Retail | Non Subscriber 20% off | Subscriber 40% off | Standing Order 50% off | Quantity | Totals |
|---|---|---|---|---|---|---|
| **General Interest** | | | | | | |
| **Nudes 1** | ☐ $40 | ☐ $32 | ☐ $24 | ☐ $20 | | |
| **Nudes 2** | ☐ $50 | ☐ $40 | ☐ $30 | ☐ $25 | | |
| **Passion & Line** | ☐ $50 | ☐ $40 | ☐ $30 | ☐ $25 | | |
| **Pool Light** | ☐ $70 | ☐ $56 | ☐ $42 | ☐ $35 | | |
| **Typography 2** | ☐ $70 | ☐ $56 | ☐ $42 | ☐ $35 | | |
| **Walter Iooss** | ☐ $70 | ☐ $56 | ☐ $42 | ☐ $35 | | |
| **Design Books** | | | | | | |
| **Apple Design** | ☐ $45 | ☐ $36 | ☐ $27 | ☐ $23 | | |
| **Bottle Design** | ☐ $40 | ☐ $32 | ☐ $24 | ☐ $20 | | |
| **Magazine Design** | ☐ $70 | ☐ $56 | ☐ $42 | ☐ $35 | | |
| **Products by Design 1** | ☐ $70 | ☐ $56 | ☐ $42 | ☐ $35 | | |
| **Products by Design 2** | ☐ $70 | ☐ $56 | ☐ $42 | ☐ $35 | | |
| **Web Design Now** | ☐ $70 | ☐ $56 | ☐ $42 | ☐ $35 | | |

Shipping & handling per book, US $ 5.00, Canada $ 10.00, Elsewhere $15.00

New York State shipments add 8.25% tax

☐ I am not a subscriber, but I want to qualify for the 20% off discount.

| **Graphis Magazine** | USA (shipping included) | Canada (shipping included) | International (shipping included) | International (airmail surcharge included) |
|---|---|---|---|---|
| One year subscription, 6 Issues | ☐ $90 | ☐ $100 | ☐ $125 | ☐ $184 |
| Two year subscription, 12 Issues | ☐ $165 | ☐ $185 | ☐ $235 | ☐ $294 |
| Student subscription, 6 Issues | ☐ $59 | ☐ $59 | ☐ $80 | ☐ $139 |

☐ I am presently a Graphis magazine subscriber and therefore, qualify for the 40% discount.

**Total**

| | |
|---|---|
| Name | ☐ American Express ☐ Visa ☐ Mastercard ☐ Check |
| Company | |
| Address | Card # |
| City State Zip | Expiration |
| Daytime phone | Card holder's signature |

Copy or send this order form and make check payable to Graphis Inc. For even faster turn-around service, or if you have any questions about subscribing call us at the following numbers in the **US (800) 209. 4234, outside the US (212) 532. 9387 ext. 242 or 241, Fax (212) 696. 4242. Graphis 141 Lexington Avenue New York, New York 10016-8193. Order Graphis on the Web from anywhere in the world: www.graphis.com**

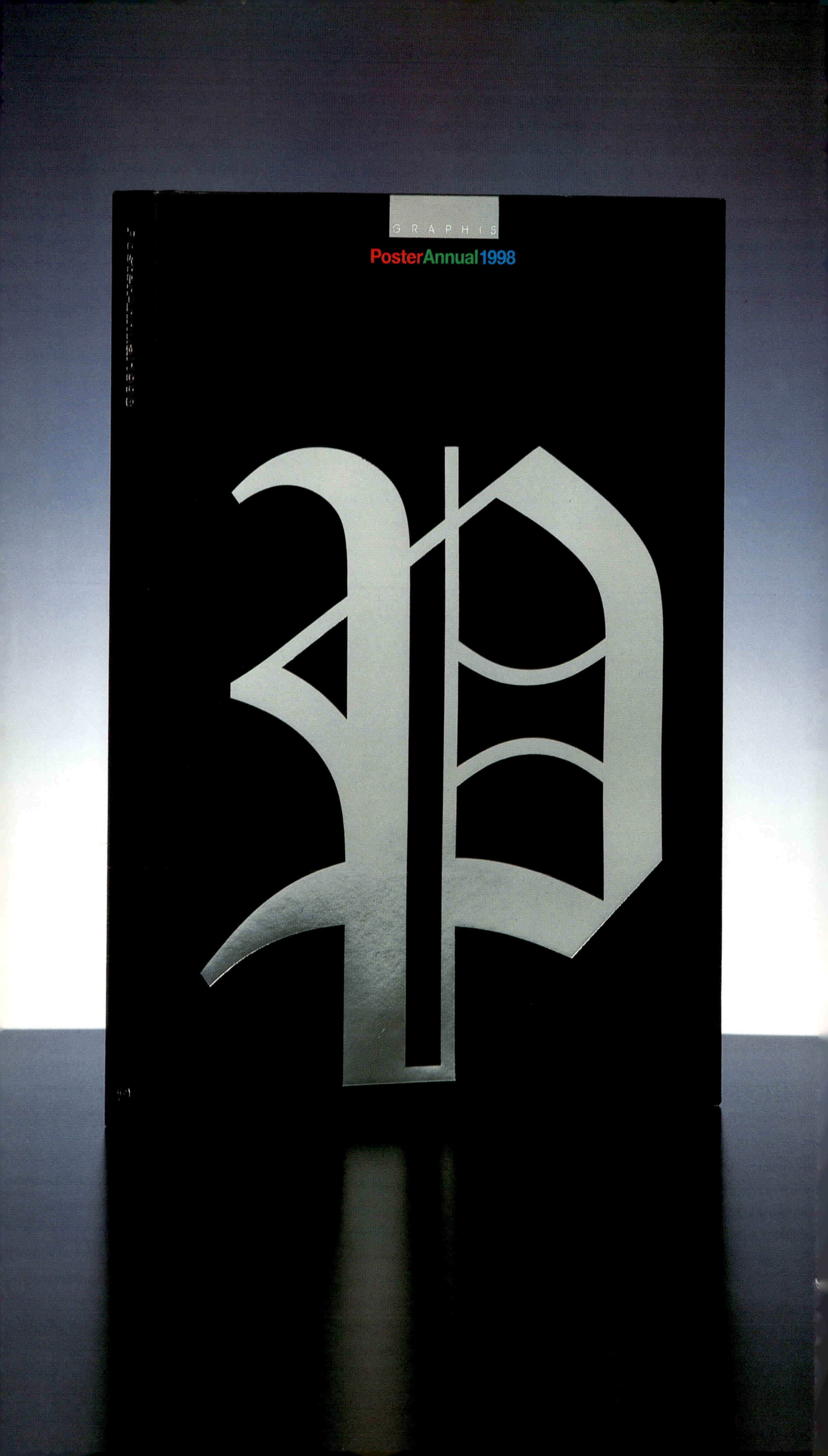
GRAPHIS
PosterAnnual1998

## Graphis Books Call For Entry

If you would like us to put you on our Call for Entries mailing list for any of our books, please fill out the form and check off the specific books of which you would like to be a part. We now consolidate our mailings twice a year for our spring and fall books. If information is needed on specific deadlines for any of our books, please consult our web site: www.graphis.com.

**Graphic Design Books**
- ☐ Advertising Annual
- ☐ Annual Reports
- ☐ Book Design
- ☐ Brochure
- ☐ Corporate Identity
- ☐ Design Annual
- ☐ Digital Fonts
- ☐ Diagrams
- ☐ Poster Annual
- ☐ Products by Design
- ☐ Letterhead
- ☐ Logo Design
- ☐ Music CD
- ☐ New Media
- ☐ Packaging
- ☐ Paper Promotions
- ☐ Typography

**Photography Books**
- ☐ Digital Photo (Professional)
- ☐ Human Con. (Photojournalism)
- ☐ New Talent (Amateur)
- ☐ Nudes (Professional)
- ☐ Nudes (Fine Art)
- ☐ Photo Annual (Professional)
- ☐ Photography (Fine Art)

**Student Books**
- ☐ Advertising Annual
- ☐ Design Annual
- ☐ Photo Annual (Professional)
- ☐ Products by Design
- ☐ **All the Books**
- ☐ All Design Books only
- ☐ All Photo Books only
- ☐ All Student Books only

First Name: ____________ Last Name: ____________

Company: ____________

Telephone: ____________ Fax: ____________

Mailing Address: ____________ City: ____________

State, Country: ____________ Zip: ____________

**Copy or mail form to : Graphis, Call for Entries, 141 Lexington Ave., New York, New York 10016-819, USA, or fax to 212. 213 3229**

Beckett™

## INTERNATIONAL PAPER: A PAPER LOVE STORY THAT BEGAN 100 YEARS AGO.

It started as a pulp and paper company based in the Northeastern part of the United States. Now, 100 years later, International Paper is a world-class company with manufacturing operations in 31 countries throughout the world.

On January 28, 1898, representatives from 17 pulp and paper mills met and agreed to form International Paper. Three days later, on January 31, the incorporation papers were filed in Albany, New York.

During its early years, International Paper was the nation's largest producer of newsprint, supplying 60 percent of all newsprint sold in the U.S. and exporting to Argentina, England and Australia.

Hugh Chisholm served as president of International Paper from 1898 to 1907 and under his leadership, the first laboratory in the American pulp and paper industry was constructed.

The Great Depression of the 1930s was a difficult period for International Paper. To help weather the hard times, International Paper introduced new products and branched out into the packaging business. International Paper was one of the first companies to manufacture linerboard on the Foudrinier. (The original Foudrinier, invented in 1799 and later perfected in 1801, allowed paper to be made in continuous rolls instead of one sheet at a time).

In 1939, International Paper pioneered bleached kraft grades for folding cartons, tags, and file folders and supplied the first bleached kraft paper grades suitable for milk carton production.

In 1941, the company simplified its structure and during World War II, International Paper converted some manufacturing operations to produce military items that included the V-1 box, which replaced wooden crates for shipping military supplies.

International Paper saw unprecedented growth and prosperity after World War II. The company had no debt and expanded its landholdings, more than doubling its fee-owned lands from 2.5 million to 5.8 million acres. To enhance forest management and research, International Paper developed its professional forestry services, established a research laboratory at Mobile, Alabama, and developed the "Super Tree" through selective breeding of genetically superior pine trees.

In 1955, the company launched a multimillion dollar research program to develop the plastic-coated milk carton. It also formed the International Paper Company Foundation, a grant-making organization that supports education in International Paper communities. Today, the foundation supports various environmental, civic, cultural, and health programs throughout the United States.

### International Expansion

International Paper expanded outside the U.S. in the late 1950s. It had been a major exporter for decades with sales in London, Paris, Zurich and Johannesburg. Still, in 1959, with over $1 billion in sales, International Paper added the first overseas manufacturing operations through joint ventures with container companies in Israel, Germany, Greece, and Italy. That same year, it organized a new subsidiary and built a liquid packaging plant in Caracas, Venezuela.

International Paper continued its international expansion throughout the 1960s and in 1969, the Corporate Research Center at Sterling Forest, New York was built.

A large scale corporate reorganization in 1976 replaced the Southern Kraft and The Northern Divisions with functional business units: white papers, consumer packaging, industrial packaging, wood products, and speciality packaging. Production managers were encouraged to think like marketing and financial managers, as well.

During the 1980s, International Paper launched a quality program that focused employees on customer needs giving them opportunities to improve product quality and to help redistribute decision-making authority throughout the organization. The company also introduced a variety of new products, including Classic Pak which captured a 20 percent share of the poultry market.

International Paper acquired Hammermill, referred to as the "best-known name in paper," which had a distribution network and reputation for quality unrivaled in the American pulp and paper industry. Its distribution network became the foundation for ResourceNet International, now called xpedx.

### The Move to Memphis

International Paper moved its headquarters to Memphis, Tennessee in 1987 to be closer to the mills and other facilities. During the 1980s, the company had strengthened its position in speciality markets by investing in businesses that were related to its core business but less cyclical in earnings than the pulp and paper market. In 1985, they took ownership of Arizona Chemical, a leading global supplier of pulp chemicals. Three years later, they acquired Maonite Corporation, a manufacturer of hardboard wood products like door facings.

As the decade came to a close, the company continued to increase its international holdings. In 1989, International Paper acquired Zanders Feinpapiere AG, Germany's leading producer of coated papers that was founded in 1829, and Aussedat Rey, a diversified French manufacturer of office copying paper, speciality panels, and related products that dated back to the 18th century.

Then in 1992, International Paper acquired Kwidzyn, Poland's most modern paper mill. This was the first acquisition in eastern Europe after the end of the Cold War.

By 1995, International Paper was a major shareholder in Carter Holt Harvey of New Zealand, which operated in New Zealand and Australia. International Paper also owns part of COPEC, a Chilean energy and forestry company.

In 1996, Federal Paper Board teamed with International Paper in a $3.5 billion transaction. Later that year, International Paper opened the new Cincinnati Technology Center that develops improvements in printing, packaging, and extrusion coating.

By 1996, sales reached $20 billion and today 85,000 employees make International Paper a global leader and a company of choice for both customers and shareholders.

In 1997, Zanders, Aussedat Rey, and Strathmore Beckett integrated their European speciality paper divisions to form a new company called International Paper Premium Papers (IPPP). The complete range of speciality products from Aussedat Rey mills at Robertsau, Strasbourg, and Lana Docelles, as well as the Zanders mills of Reflex and Gohrmühle form the group. Yet, the American Strathmore Beckett products are still offered as an independent franchise from their European headquarters in the Netherlands.

International Paper is committed to becoming an organization with a strong customer focus and a greater degree of teamwork in order to satisfy customers and stay ahead of the competition. As Chairman John Dillon said recently,"I can think of no other company in the industry with more capacities to meet these objectives than ours. We are proud of what we have achieved in 100 years and look forward to greater success in the future."

## INTERNATIONAL PAPER: HUNDERT JAHRE LIEBE ZUM PAPIER

Alles begann mit einer Zellstoff- und Papierfirma im Nordosten der Vereinigten Staaten. Heute, 100 Jahre später, ist International Paper ein Unternehmen der Weltklasse mit Produktionsstandorten in 31 Ländern rund um die Welt.

Am 28. Januar 1898 trafen sich Vertreter von 17 Zellstoff- und Papierfabriken und vereinbarten die Gründung von International Paper. Drei Tage später, am 31. Januar 1898, wurde das Unternehmen in Albany im Staat New York angemeldet.

In den ersten Jahren war International Paper der größte amerikanische Hersteller von Zeitungspapier mit einem Marktanteil von 60 Prozent, wobei auch nach Argentinien, England und Australien exportiert wurde.

Von 1898 bis 1907 war Hugh Chisholm Präsident von International Paper. Unter seiner Führung wurde das erste Labor der amerikanischen Zellstoff- und Papierindustrie gebaut.

Die große Depression in den dreißiger Jahren war auch für International Paper eine schwere Zeit. Um sich in dieser schwierigen Lage zu behaupten, führte International Paper damals neue Produkte ein und diversifizierte in das Verpackungsgeschäft. Dabei gehörte International Paper zu den ersten Firmen, die kaschierten Karton auf der Foudrinier-Maschine herstellten. (Mit der Foudrinier-Maschine, die 1799 erfunden und 1801 weiterentwickelt wurde, konnte Papier erstmalig in durchlaufenden Rollen statt jeweils nur in einem Bogen hergestellt werden.)

1939 war International Paper wegweisend mit gebleichten Kraftpapiersorten zur Herstellung von Faltschachteln, Etiketten und Aktenordnern und lieferte die ersten gebleichten Kraftpapiersorten, die für die Produktion von Milchtüten geeignet waren.

Nach dem Krieg erfuhr International Paper ein noch nie dagewesenes Wachstum und einen beispiellosen Wohlstand. Das Unternehmen hatte keine Schulden und verdoppelte seinen Grundbesitz von 1 Million Hektar auf 2,3 Millionen Hektar. Zur Verbesserung der Forstverwaltung und -forschung entwickelte International Paper einen eigenen professionellen Forstbereich, errichtete in Mobile, Alabama ein Forschungslabor und entwickelte den „Superbaum" durch selektive Zucht genetisch überlegener Nadelbäume.

1955 startete das Unternehmen ein Forschungsprogramm mit einem Budget von vielen Millionen Dollar für die Entwicklung der kunststoffbeschichteten Milchtüte. Zusätzlich wurde die International Paper Company Foundation gegründet, eine Stiftung zur Förderung der Bildung in den Standortgemeinden von International Paper. Heute finanziert die Stiftung vielfältige Programme im Bereich Umwelt, Soziales, Kultur und Gesundheit in den gesamten USA.

**Internationale Expansion**

In den späten fünfziger Jahren expandierte International Paper auch außerhalb den Vereinigten Staaten. Seit Jahrzehnten war der Export ein wichtiger Umsatzfaktor, besonders nach London, Paris, Zürich und Johannesburg. Im Jahre 1959, als International Paper einen Jahresumsatz von über einer Milliarde Dollar hatte, wurden mit Behälterfirmen in Israel, Deutschland, Griechenland und Italien Gemeinschaftsunternehmen und somit die ersten Fertigungsstätten im Ausland gegründet. Im gleichen Jahr wurde eine neue Tochtergesellschaft eröffnet und eine Verpackungsanlage für Flüssigbehälter in Caracas in Venezuela errichtet.

Die internationale Expansion von International Paper wurde in den sechziger Jahren fortgeführt. 1969 wurde das Forschungszentrum des Konzerns in Sterling Forest im Staat New York gebaut.

Im Jahre 1976 wurden die Sparten Southern Kraft und Northern durch die folgenden Funktionsbereiche ersetzt: Weißpapier, Komsumverpackung, Industrieverpackung, Holzprodukte und Spezialverpackung. Die Produktionsleiter waren angewiesen, sich auch die Denkweise von Marketing- und Finanzmanagern anzueignen. In den achziger Jahren startete International Paper ein Qualitätsprogramm, das die Mitarbeiter auf die Bedürfnisse der Kunden ausrichtete, den Mitarbeitern die Möglichkeit zur Verbesserung bot und dazu beitrug, die Entscheidungsfindung auf das gesamte Unternehmen zu verlagern. Weiterhin führte das Unternehmen mehrere Neuprodukte ein, zum Beispiel Classic Pak, das 20 Prozent des Geflügelmarktes eroberte.

International Paper erwarb Hammermill, das den Ruf des „am besten bekannten Papiernamens" besitzt und für das überlegene Vertriebsnetz und die herausragende Qualität in der amerikanischen Papier- und Zellstoffindustrie berühmt ist. Das Vertriebsnetz von Hammermill wurde der Grundstein für die Firma ResourceNet International, die ab 1. Januar 1998 unter xpedx firmiert.

**Umzug nach Memphis**

Im Jahre 1987 verlegte International Paper die Konzernzentrale nach Memphis, um näher bei den Papierfabriken und den anderen Werken zu sein.

Das Unternehmen stärkte in den achziger Jahren seine Position auf Spezialmärkten, indem gezielt in Firmen investiert wurde, die mit dem Kerngeschäft des Konzerns zu tun hatten, jedoch weniger konjunkturabhängig als der Zellstoff- und Papiermarkt waren. 1985 übernahm International Paper die Firma Arizona Chemical, ein weltweit führender Lieferant von Zellstoffchemikalien. Drei Jahre später folgte der Kauf der Maonite Corporation, die Holzfaserplatten-produkte wie z.B. Türverkleidungen herstellt.

Am Ende des Jahrzehnts folgten internationale Übernahmen. 1989 wurde Zanders Feinpapiere AG, der führende deutsche Hersteller von gestrichenen Papieren, sowie Aussedat Rey, ein diversifizierter französischer Produzent von Kopierpapier, Spezialplatten und ähnlichen Produkten, erworben. Zanders wurde 1829 gegründet, während die Anfänge von Aussedat Rey bereits im 18. Jahrhunders liegen.

Am Ende 1996 erzielte International Paper einen Umsatz von 20 Milliarden Dollar. Heute ist International Paper mit 85.000 Mitarbeitern ein Weltführer der Branche und sowohl für Kunden als auch Aktionäre eine erste Adresse.

1997 bildeten Zanders, Aussedat Rey und Strathmore Beckett in Europa mit ihren Spezialpapierbereichen ein neues Unternehmen namens International Paper Premium Papers (IPPP). Die gesamte Palette von Spezialprodukten der Papierfabriken von Aussedat Rey in Robertsau, Straßburg und Lana Docelles sowie die Reflex- und Gohrsmühle-Fabriken von Zanders wird die Gruppe bilden. Die Produkte der amerikanischen Hersteller Strathmore und Beckett werden weiterhin unabhängig von der europäischen Zentrale in Holland vertrieben.

International Paper hat sich das Ziel gesetzt, ein kundenorientiertes Unternehmen mit mehr Teamarbeit zu werden, um so Kunden-wünsche erfüllen und den Wettbewerb schlagen zu können. So sagte der Vorstand John Dillon neulich: „Ich kenne kein anderes Unternehmen in der Branche, das diese Ziele besser erreichen könnte als wir. Wir sind stolz darauf, was wir in 100 Jahren erreicht haben, und freuen uns auf einen noch größeren Erfolg in der Zukunft."

## INTERNATIONAL PAPER: UNE HISTOIRE D'AMOUR AVEC LE PAPIER QUI A COMMENCÉ VOICI UN SIÈCLE

Tout commence avec une manufacture de pâte et de papier située dans le nord-est des Etats-Unis. Aujourd'hui, 100 ans plus tard, International Paper est une société d'envergure mondiale qui possède des sites de fabrication dans 31 pays du monde.

Le 28 janvier 1898, les représentants de 17 manufactures de pâte et de papier se réunissent et tombent d'accord pour créer International Paper. Trois jours plus tard, le 31 janvier, la société nouvellement formée est enregistrée à Albany, New York.

Au cours de ses premières années d'activité, International Paper est le principal fabricant de papier journal du pays. En effet, il fournit 60 % du papier journal vendu aux Etats-Unis et exporte vers l'Argentine, la Grande-Bretagne et l'Australie.

Hugh Chisholm préside International Paper de 1898 à 1907 et c'est à cette époque que l'on construit le premier laboratoire de l'industrie américaine de la pâte et du papier.

Pendant la Grande Crise des années 30, International Paper connaît une période difficile. Pour parvenir à surmonter la tempête, International Paper lance de nouveaux produits et se diversifie dans le secteur de l'emballage. International Paper est une des premières entreprises à fabriquer des cartons sur le Foudrinier. (Le Foudrinier d'origine, inventé en 1799 et perfectionné en 1801, permet de produire le papier en rouleaux et non plus feuille par feuille).

En 1939, International Paper commercialise pour la première fois du papier kraft blanchi de qualité supérieure pour cartons pliables, étiquettes et porte-documents et fournit le premier papier kraft blanchi adapté à la fabrications des emballages de lait.

International Paper connaît une croissance et une prospérité exceptionnelles après la Seconde Guerre. L'entreprise n'a pas une seule dette et fait plus que doubler ses biens fonciers puisqu'ils passent de 2,5 millions à 5,8 millions d'acres (n.d.t. : 1 acre = 0,405 hectares). Pour améliorer la gestion des forêts et la recherche, International Paper développe ses services forestiers professionnels, établit un laboratoire de recherches à Mobile, Alabama et met au point le „super tree" par croisements sélectifs d'espèces de pins supérieures.

En 1955, la société lance un programme de recherches qui porte sur plusieurs millions de Dollars pour mettre au point un emballage de lait en carton doublé de matière plastique. Elle fonde également la Paper Company Foundation, un organisme chargé d'attribuer des bourses d'étude dans les communes où elle est implantée. Aujourd'hui, la Fondation supporte différents projets dans le secteur de l'environnement, de la vie civile, dans le domaine de la culture et de la santé à travers les Etats-Unis.

### Expansion internationale

International Paper développe ses activités hors des Etats-Unis à la fin des années 50. Société exportatrice de tout premier plan pendant des décennies, International Paper a des point de vente à Londres, Paris, Zurich et Johannesbourg. En 1959, alors que ses ventes atteignent plus de 1 milliard de Dollars, la société acquiert ses premiers sites de fabrication outre-mer par le biais de joint ventures en Israël, Allemagne, Grèce et Italie. La même année, elle crÈe une nouvelle filiale et construit une usine de conditionnement des liquides à Caracas, Venezuela. International Paper poursuit son expansion internationale tout au long des années 60. En 1969, elle construit le Corporate Research Center à Sterling Forest, N.Y.

Une vaste opération de restructuration conduit, en 1976, au remplacement de Southern Kraft et des Northern Divisions par des unités fonctionnelles correspondant aux secteur suivants : papier blanc, conditionnement consommateur, conditionnement industriel, produits en bois et emballages spéciaux. Les directeurs de production sont invités à ne pas oublier les aspects commerciaux et financiers. Au cours des années 80, International Paper lance un programme qualité qui attire l'attention des collaborateurs sur les besoins du consommateur, leur donne la possibilité d'améliorer la qualité des produits et encourage la prise de décisions à tous les échelons de l'organisation. La société introduit également toute une variété de nouveaux produits, y compris Classic Pak qui conquiert 20 % du marché de la volaille.

International Paper achète Hammermill, encore appelée „le meilleur nom du papier," avec son réseau de distribution et sa réputation de qualité inégalée dans l'industrie américaine de la pâte et du papier. Son réseau de distribution met en place le ResourceNet International, en vigueur depuis le 1er janvier 1998 sous le nom de xpedx.

### Le déménagement à Memphis

International Paper établit son quartier général à Memphis en 1987 pour se rapprocher des manufactures et des autres équipements.

La société renforce sa position sur le marché des spécialités au cours de années 80 en investissant dans des affaires liées à son activité principale mais moins sujettes aux fluctuations cycliques que la pâte et le papier. En 1985, elle acquiert Arizona Chemical, un des premiers fournisseurs de produits chimiques pour la pâte à papier. Trois ans plus tard, elle achète la Masonite Corporation qui fabrique des panneaux durs pour parements de portes, par exemple.

Vers la fin de la décennie, la société continue à accroître ses possessions internationales. En 1989, International Paper reprend Zanders Feinpapiere AG, le premier producteur allemand de papiers couchés et Aussedat Rey, un fabriquant français de papiers de tirage à usage de bureau, de plusieurs gammes de spécialités et de produits annexes. Zanders a été fondé en 1829 alors que la naissance de Aussedat Rey remonte au 18e siècle.

En 1996, les ventes atteignent 20 milliards de Dollars et aujourd'hui, 85 000 collaborateurs font de International Paper un leader universel et une entreprise de tout premier choix pour les clients et les actionnaires.

En 1997, Zanders, Aussedat Rey et Strathmore Beckett unissent leurs secteurs européens des spécialités de papier pour former une nouvelle société appelée International Paper Premium Papers (IPPP).

La gamme complète des spécialités de la manufacture Aussedat Rey à Robertsau, Strasbourg et Lana Docelles, ainsi que la manufacture Zanders de Reflex et Gohrmühle constitueront le groupe. Les produits américains de Strathmore Beckett sont toujours proposés en franchise indépendante par le quartier général européen situé aux Pays-Bas.

International Paper est destinée à devenir une organisation largement orientée vers les consommateurs et à renforcer son esprit d'équipe pour satisfaire les clients et devancer la concurrence. Comme le disait récemment son Président John Dillon : „Je ne vois aucune autre entreprise industrielle qui posséderait plus d'atouts que nous pour réaliser ces objectifs. Nous sommes fiers de ce que nous avons obtenus en 100 ans et nous nous attendons à un succès encore plus grand à l'avenir."

## BECKETT PAPERS - INNOVATION IS THE KEY TO SUCCESS

Founded in 1848 by William Beckett, the son of an early Ohio settler, Beckett is the fourth oldest operating fine paper mill in the United States; a true industry pioneer.

In the years to follow, Beckett Papers take credit for an unequaled list of industry innovations. The first premium lithographic paper, the first fluorescent lithographic paper, first use of currugated cartons, first use of polyethylene-lined cartons, and first use of polyethylene wrap on skids are among such innovations.

Beckett´s innovation did not stop with the acquisition of the mill by Hammermill Paper in 1959. First came the introduction of the industry of lightweight duplex papers. Next, in 1970, Beckett took advantage of its expertise in embossing and introduced a comprehensive line of linen printing and writing papers-Cambric. Beckett continued its innovations in embossing during the 1980´s with introductions of the grade lines Ridge and Enhance!.

In 1986 the Hammermill Paper Group was acquired by the world´s largest paper producer: International Paper. The vast resources of International Paper allows Beckett to continue its rich tradition of innovations. In 1991, Beckett Papers was the first fine paper mill to manufacture its complete product line with recycled fiber.

Nowadays, Beckett Papers maintains a modern plant with three paper machines, rewinding and laminating capabilities, and a large finishing department. The mill can produce more than 250,000 different products, in an assortment of weights, finishes, and colours.

Beckett papers are sold by independent wholesale paper merchants in every major city in North America as well as in many European countries. All merchants have the exclusive sales rights for their country.

**PRODUCT LINES**

Beckett's environmental awareness is evident in most of its contemporary line-up of six premium grades, each of which includes recycled fibre content. The mill combines at least 50% recycled content (10% post consumer) with the highest standards of product quality.

**Beckett grades:**

- Cambric: with a premium linen finish
- R.S.V.P.: a true felt finish for prestigious look and feel
- Ridge: deeply grooved finish that adds a look of distinction
- Enhance!: with a satiny finish and contemporary colour palette
- Concept: versatile with three finishes and environmental appeal
- Beckett Expression: an affordable premium paper with 24% post consumer waste content and a smooth finish that invites ink coverage

**Marketing activities**

- The mill operates the Beckett Idea Center as a resource for complete projects accomplished with Becketts Papers. "Great ideas demand great papers" the Beckett motto attests. With courteous service, paper samples, and promotions the center is a valuable creative resource that demonstrates the printability of Beckett papers.
- Merchant Specification Conference: Specification representatives from the States and Europe are provided with information on the role of paper in graphic design. They also receive a lot of useful hints on how Beckett papers can be promoted successfully. The conference is held once a year and lasts for three days.
- Promotional Items: Beckett Papers prints samples, both in-house designs and commercial, to give designers some inspiration for creative paper use. These samples are welcome in ad agencies and are handed out and explained by the graphic art consultants of the paper merchants.
- Beckett honors award: This is a competition which is held twice a year, in June and December. Judging for each contest takes place in different host cities and is conducted by a panel of designers, printers, and merchant art consultants. Three winners are named in two categories- business communication and general. All winning entries will receive Beckett Honors´Tiffany crystal stars to commemorate the event. Individual crystal stars will be awarded to the designer, printer, and end user of each piece. Entries from all over the world will be judged.

**THE BECKETT GRADES**

**Enhance!**

A pretty name for a pretty paper. No question. Merely the embossing turns each sheet into a material of which dreams are made. Light and bright, warm and comforting, capricious lovers of beautiful paper choose Enhance! in any one of the five mediterranian marble shades.

**R.S.V.P.**

Close your eyes and enjoy this paper as a sensorial treat. It is extraordinary thick, but maintains a smoothness which runs like cream through your fingers. And then, the look: very distinctive, very honest, and with fine color nuances. One appreciates the tranquil silence of this tactile experience.

**Ridge**

Ridged- that is exactly what the paper´s embossing looks like. Ridged with clear, linear parrallels, which gives the paper a cool and technical elegance. A thrilling contrast is the smooth surface of the paper which takes away all severity from the linear pattern. Another suprise is the smooth back. Ridge has got more than just one good side.

**Expression**

Startling at the beginning, these natural clear colors- a sunny winter afternoon cast into paper. The first touch is almost a shock–so incredibly soft, so incredibly smooth. What a material to design on. It is hard to beleive that it contains 50% recovered fibres. Without hesitation, the hand touches once more, an impression of Expression.

**Cambric**

A paper like Irish linen: strong, fine, and high-quality. The wide variety of colors and embossings make it possible for Cambric to always appear new and different. As a letterhead paper–in discreet colors and simple design–it gives the impression of success. With loud colors and interesting fibres it gives the perfect background for a private letter that looks alltogether differerent.

## BECKETT PAPERS - INNOVATION HEISST DER SCHLÜSSEL ZUM ERFOLG

Beckett wurde 1848 von William Beckett, dem Sohn eines frühen Siedlers in Ohio, gegründet und ist damit als Pionier der Branche die viertälteste Feinpapierfabrik in den Ver-einigten Staaten.

Seit das Unternehmen besteht, kann Beckett Papers eine unvergleichliche Reihe von Innovationen in der Papierbranche vorweisen. Zu diesen Innovationen gehören das erste hochwertige Lithografiepapier, das erste fluoreszierende Lithografiepapier, der erste Einsatz von Wellpappe, von mit PE-Film ausgekleideten Kartons und von PE-folienverschweißten Ladegestellen.

Hammermill Paper erwarb die Fabrik 1959 und setzte diese Entwicklung fort. Zuerst wurden leichte Duplexpapiere eingeführt. 1970 konnte Beckett auf ihre Erfahrung im Prägen zurückgreifen und führte ein umfangreiches Programm von leinengeprägten Druck- und Schreibpapieren ein - Cambric. Diese Prägeinnovationen wurden in den achtziger Jahren mit der Einführung der Qualitätssorten Ridge und Enhance! fortgeführt.

1986 wurde der Hammermill Paper Konzern von International Paper, dem weltweit größten Papierhersteller, erworben. Dank der hohen Ressourcen von International Paper konnte Beckett das bereits bekannte Innovationsstreben weiterführen: Im Jahre 1991 war Beckett der erste Feinpapierhersteller, der seine Produktpalette aus wiederverwerteten Fasern herstellte. Heute unterhält Beckett Papers eine moderne Fabrik mit drei Papiermaschinen, Umroll- und Kaschiereinrichtungen sowie eine große Veredelungsabteilung. Die Fabrik kann über 250.000 verschiedene Produkte in verschiedenen Gewichten, Oberflächen und Farben herstellen.

Beckett Papiere werden über unabhängige Papiergroßhändler in jeder wichtigen Stadt in Nordamerika sowie in vielen europäischen Ländern vertrieben. Alle Händler haben für ihr Land das Alleinverkaufsrecht.

**PRODUKTLINIEN**

Das Umweltbewußtsein von Beckett ist bei den meisten Papierqualitäten der heutigen Produktpalette sichtbar, die allesamt einen Anteil wiederverwendeter Fasern haben. Mindestens 50 Prozent Recyclingfasern (10% post consumer) werden in der Papierfabrik mit dem höchsten Qualitätsmaßstab kombiniert.

**Die Qualitäten von Beckett:**

- Cambric: mit hochwertiger Leinenstruktur
- R.S.V.P.: eine Filzoberfläche, Genuß für Augen und Hände
- Ridge: edle Ausstrahlung dank gerillter Oberfläche
- Enhance!: mit einer Satinstruktur und moderner Farbauswahl
- Concept: vielseitig mit drei Oberflächenstrukturen mit Umweltcharakter
- Beckett Expression: günstiges Qualitätspapier mit 24 Prozent Altpapieranteil und einer glatten Oberfläche, die Tinte gut aufnimmt

**Marketingaktivitäten**

- Die Papierfabrik unterhält das Beckett Idea Center als Fundus für mit Beckett Papieren gedruckte Muster. Das Motto von Beckett verspricht „Gutes Papier für gute Ideen". Das Center bietet mit dem freundlichen Service, Papiermustern und Verkaufsförderungs-maßnahmen kreative Ideen, die die Bedruckbarkeit der Papiersorten von Beckett unter Beweis stellen.
- Händlerkonferenz: Die Vertreter aus den Vereinigten Staaten und Europa erhalten auf dieser Konferenz sehr viele Informationen über die Rolle des Papiers in der Grafikbranche sowie nützliche Tips, wie das Papier von Beckett erfolgreich vermarktet werden kann. Die dreitätige Konferenz findet einmal pro Jahr statt.
- Druckmuster: Beckett Papers druckt viele Proben, die selbst oder extern gestaltet werden, um den Designern Inspirationen zur kreativen Nutzung von Papier zu geben. Diese kostenlosen Proben werden gerne von Werbeagenturen angenommen und von den Grafikberatern der Papierhändler erklärt.
- Beckett honors award: Dieser Wettbewerb findet in verschiedenen Städten zweimal jährlich im Juni bzw. Dezember statt. Die Preisrichter sind Designer, Drucker und Grafikberater der Händler. In den beiden Kategorien „Werbung" und „Allgemeines" werden jeweils drei Gewinner benannt. Alle Gewinner erhalten die „Tiffany-Kristallsterne" als Erinnerung an dieses Ereignis. Dem Designer, Drucker und Endverbraucher jedes prämierten Stückes werden einzelne Sterne verliehen. Teilnehmer aus der ganzen Welt sind zum Wettbewerb eingeladen.

**BECKETT - DIE PAPIERQUALITÄTEN**

**Expression**

13 klare natürliche Farben in zwei Gewichten und die ungewöhnlich zarte, samtige Oberfläche zeichnen diese Qualität aus. Expression besteht zu 50 % aus wiederverwendeten Rohstoffen und eignet sich sehr gut für alle Druckverfahren. Das Angebot wird ergänzt durch passende Briefhüllen, Expression ist damit bestens für einen vielseitigen Einsatz gerüstet. R.S.V.P. Die authentische Filzmarkierung verleiht diesem Papier sein unverwechsel-bares Aussehen und die voluminöse Haptik.

**R.S.V.P.**

eignet sich als Auflagenpapier, aber auch sehr gut als Umschlagqualität, es ist bis 270 g/qm erhältlich. Die Wahl zwischen den13 fein nuancierten Farben fällt schwer; das fertige Druckergebnis wird jeden Empfänger begeistern, der auf Natürlichkeit und Individualität Wert legt.

**Ridge**

Furche - das ist die deutsche Entsprechung für Ridge. So sieht die Prägung des Papieres aus, es ist von klaren linearen Parallelen durchfurcht. In Kombination mit der samtigen Oberfläche ist das ein reizvoller Kontrast und gibt dem Papier eine kühle Eleganz. 8 Farben und zwei Gewichte bieten die ideale Grundlage für viele Gestaltungsmöglichleiten.

**Enhance**

Enhance - Verschönerung, ein guter Name für ein schönes Papier. Die zarte stoffähnliche Oberflächenprägung kommt in außergewöhnlich hellen oder warmen Farbtönen daher. Einige davon tragen eine mediterran anmutende Marmorschattierung.

**Cambric**

Ein Papier, das die Anmutung von irischem Leinen hat. Eine breite Farbpalette ermöglicht einen vielfätigen Einsatz. Als gediegenes Geschäftspapier hat Cambric einen ebenso perfekten Auftritt wie als freche Privatpost in knallbunten Farben oder mit melierten Fasern.

Sämtliche Qualitäten sind über den Feinpapiergroßhandel zu beziehen. Dort gibt es auch Muster für Layouts oder Andrucke.

## BECKETT PAPERS - INNOVATION EST LA CLÉ DU SUCCÈS

La société fut fondée en 1848 par William Beckett, fils d'un colon très tôt établi dans l'Ohio. Beckett est la quatrième parmi les plus anciennes manufactures de papier surfin encore en opération aux Etats-Unis. Elle fait figure de véritable pionnier du secteur industriel.

Au cours des années qui suivent sa fondation, Beckett Papers produit une quantité inégalable d'innovations dont voici quelques exemples : le premier papier de qualité supérieure pour impression lithographique, le premier papier fluorescent pour impression lithographique, la première utilisation du carton ondulé, la première utilisation de carton garni de polyéthylène et la première utilisation d'une feuille de polyéthylène pour la protection des casiers de stockage.

Rachetée par Hammermill Paper en 1959, Beckett ne cesse pas pour autant de lancer des nouveautés sur le marché. Citons, en premier lieu, l'introduction des papiers duplex légers. Puis, en 1970, avantagée par l'avance qu'elle possède dans le domaine du gaufrage, la société Beckett est la première à proposer une gamme diversifiée de papier toilé et de papier à lettres qui reçoit le nom de Cambric. Beckett continue d'innover dans le domaine du gaufrage au cours des années 80 en lançant les séries de qualité supérieure Ridge et Enhance.

En 1986, le Hammermill Paper Group est racheté par le plus grand fabricant de papier du monde : International Paper. Les vastes ressources de International Paper permettent à Beckett de rester fidèle à sa tradition innovatrice. En 1991, Beckett Papers est le premier à utiliser des fibres recyclées pour toute sa ligne de produits.

Aujourd'hui, Beckett Papers possède une usine moderne abritant trois machines à papier, des équipements d'enroulage et de contrecollage ainsi qu'un grand atelier de finissage. La manufacture produit plus de 250 000 produits différents, dans un assortiment de poids, d'apprêts et de couleurs.

**Lignes de produits**

Beckett est une société soucieuse de préserver l'environnement, ce qui se traduit dans la plupart de ses six lignes de produits de qualité supérieure qui contiennent toutes des fibres recyclées. La manufacture allie une teneur minimum de 50 % de produits recyclés (10 % post consommateur) aux exigences de qualité les plus sévères.

**Les qualités Beckett :**

•Cambric : un apprêt toilé de première qualité

•R.S.V.P. : un apprêt feutré authentique pour un aspect et un toucher prestigieux

•Ridge : structure à rainures profondes qui ajoute une note distinguée

•Enhance!: un apprêt satiné et une palette de couleurs contemporaines

•Concept: polyvalent avec trois finitions et un souci réel de l'environnement

•Beckett Expression : un papier de qualité supérieur contenant 24 % de déchets post consommateur, dont l'apprêt velouté invite à l'écriture, proposé à un prix abordable

**Activités de marketing**

•La manufacture gère le Beckett Idea Center qui regroupe les projets réalisés sur les papiers Beckett. Le slogan le dit bien „Les grandes idées méritent un grand papier". Avec un service courtois, des échantillons de papier et des campagnes promotionnelles, ce centre est une source de créativité très précieuse qui démontre les qualités des impressions obtenues avec les papiers Beckett.

•Merchant Specification Conference: les agents responsables des caractéristiques techniques pour les Etats-Unis et l'Europe apprennent une foule de choses concernant le rôle du papier dans la conception graphique. Ils obtiennent également une multitude de renseignements utiles à une promotion réussie des papiers Beckett. La conférence se tient une fois par an et dure trois jours.

•Articles promotionnels : Beckett Papers imprime une multitude d'échantillons, de conception interne ou externe, pour aider les designers dans leurs recherches d'idées nouvelles appliquées au papier. Ces échantillons sont très bien accueillis par les agences de publicité. Ils sont distribués (gratuitement) et commentés par les conseillers artistiques des grossistes.

•Beckett honors award : il s'agit d'un concours qui a lieu deux fois par an, en juin et en décembre. Les compétitions se déroulent dans différentes villes sous l'autorité d'un jury composé de designers, d'imprimeurs et des conseillers artistiques des négociants. Trois lauréats sont désignés dans deux catégories - communication commerciale et domaine général. Tous les produits retenus reçoivent la récompense du Beckett Honors : les étoiles de cristal Tiffany pour commémorer l'événement. Des étoiles de cristal individuelles sont remises aux designers, imprimeurs et utilisateurs de chaque article. Les produits du monde entier sont admis à participer au concours.

**BECKETT - LES QUALITÉS DE PAPIER**

**Expression**

13 coloris naturels disponibles en deux poids et une surface particulièrement douce et veloutée caractérisent cette qualité de papier. Expression est composé à 50 % de matières premières recyclées et se prête fort bien à tous les processus d'impression. L'offre est enrichie d'enveloppes assorties. Expression est donc parfaitement adapté à une utilisation diversifiée.

**R.S.V.P.**

L'authenticité de sa marque de feutre donne à ce papier son aspect inimitable et une agréable sensation d'épaisseur au toucher. R.S.V.P. peut être employé comme papier d'édition mais également sans problème pour couvrir les brochures. Son poids peut aller jusqu'à 270 g/m2. Le choix entre 13 coloris aux nuances subtiles est difficile ; tous ceux qui attachent de l'importance à l'aspect naturel et à l'individualité seront enthousiasmés par sa qualité d'impression.

**Ridge**

Nervure - tel est l'équivalent français de Ridge. C'est d'ailleurs ainsi que se présente ce papier parcouru de nervures longitudinales parallèles. Combinées au velouté de la surface, elles produisent un contraste séduisant qui donne au papier sa sobre élégance. 8 coloris et deux poids sont un point de départ idéal à la créativité.

**Enhance!**

Enhance - embellissement, quel nom magnifique pour un beau papier. La fine structure de surface qui évoque une étoffe affiche des tons clairs ou chauds. Certains d'entre eux présentent une marbrure aux réminiscences méditerranéennes.

**Cambric**

Un papier aux allures de lin irlandais. Sa large palette de coloris permet un emploi diversifié. Sous sa version classique destinée à la correspondance commerciale, Cambric produit tout autant d'effet que dans les couleurs éclatantes ou avec les fibres chinées réservées à une correspondance privée plus désinvolte.

## STRATHMORE - BECAUSE PAPER IS PART OF THE PICTURE

When Horace Moses founded the Mittineague Paper Company in West Springfield, Massachusetts back in 1892, the memories of the Wild West were still fresh in the minds of many. Perhaps that is why he named his paper factory–Mittineague–after an Indian tribe which had once inhabited the area.

Moses' company philosophy was just as simple as it was convincing: He wanted to produce unusually high quality paper and offer an outstanding service. He was constantly searching for new paper machines with which he could manufacture unusual types of paper. He had heard that there was a machine in England that could produce deckle-edges similar to those of handmade paper. He travelled to Europe and not only did he find the machine but also a name for his products in Scotland: Strathmore.

The picturesque valley of Strathmore with its heather and Scottish thistles in full bloom left a lasting impression on Moses. In 1898, he registered the name "Strathmore" as a trademark and chose the thistle as his company's logo.

Horace Moses was convinced that he could sell his products well if he were to display the beauty of his paper in many different ways. And so he went down in American design history as the publisher of the first sample book with practical examples. For this purpose, he employed his own printer in his company: Will Bradley, who later became renowned the world over as a typography designer and printer of high quality books.

The customers were thrilled with the sample books and the paper too. The company expanded. New acquisitions included an envelope factory which ensured that there were matching envelopes for the different paper types, and all of famous Strathmore quality.

Horace Moses died in 1947 at age 85. He left a legacy, but the following management generations were not always gifted with his keen business sense. In 1962, Strathmore was sold to Hammermill and since 1986 has belonged to the largest paper conglomerate in the world: International Paper.

### THE PRODUCT RANGE

Today, Strathmore is a leading supplier in three special areas:

#### Paper containing cotton

In paper with a 25% share of cotton, Strathmore is market leader in the USA. This is predominantly due to the Strathmore Writing System. Originally developed at the end of the eighties, this system was recently revised and adapted to market conditions. Thanks to technical improvements, the paper can be used without any problems on all laser printers. In addition to different degrees of white, the colour selection also includes neutral shades which are produced using a high content of recycled material. These colours give the impression of coloured paper but can be as flexibly used as white paper.

#### Text and cover papers

Strathmore is known above all for its coloured envelope qualities. Authentic felt marks are the trademark of this paper factory. The qualities Grandee, Americana, Fiesta and Pastelle are still manufactured on the old paper machines which almost work at a manual pace. Many factories have already given up this technology in favor of faster production processes. Strathmore, in contrast, is constantly working on adapting these special features to the demands of the modern market.

#### Artist's paper

Strathmore is also the market leader in the USA for artist's paper. This paper is offered in a range stretching from 100% cotton paper to types made fully out of wood.

This paper can be bought solely in the USA through specialist retailers in sheets or as artist's blocks.

#### A modern marketing concept

Strathmore's main target is the graphic design community, which plays a decisive role in choosing paper and expresses great interest in new paper qualities and application examples. The trend is moving away from pure sample books towards combined sample and application books. The latter show examples with different printing techniques: thermography, blind blocking, foil laminating, and dye stamping. Unusual impressions can thus be attained on weighty natural papers. The application books include detailed technical information with regard to lithography, printing, and further processing. The advantage of this system is obvious: it provides a huge source of ideas without the risk of taking a shot in the dark when putting them into practice.

Strathmore also provides specialist advice to avoid that "shot in the dark." Since 1958, Strathmore has been training the "Graphic Arts Consultants" of the sales partners, paper wholesalers in 35 countries around the world. Strathmore provides a seminar, lasting several days, which teaches the agency consultants about the role of paper in graphic design, different printing techniques, as well as the latest trends in paper and design. Special consultants often provide advertising agencies with ideas and information which the printers cannot provide due to a lack of time or in-depth knowledge.

Strathmore caters to the needs of the advertising agencies in its product range. A complete program is offered for every type of paper, i.e several different weights of paper and card, as well as envelopes and matching stickers.

Strathmore's European headquarters is located in Bussum in the Netherlands. From this location the European wholesalers receive sales support especially matched to their market. As the headquarters has its own warehouse, products can be delivered within a few days.

#### The newest trends

Extensive market research has shown what people really want with paper, what trends will continue through 2000. Emphasis is of course placed on environmental friendliness. This is why at Strathmore, depending on the quality required, only paper with a maximum recycling content is produced. The use of cotton is also ecologically sound, as this is a raw material which grows back quickly. And what's more, in paper production, only the outer layers of cotton unsuitable for textile production are used. Another trend is that paper has to meet the demands of modern office printers and state-of-the-art fast printing machines. To this end, a relatively smooth closed surface and a special moisture content are required and the paper should also be available in A4 format. And last but not least, the advertising agencies require that high quality paper be affordable. The result of these findings has a name at Strathmore: Elements–an environmentally friendly composition of materials (60% recycling share), factory guaranteed suitability for laser printers (up to 105 g/m2), and a cost of about 10% less than comparable papers.

Elements was developed by product manager Bob Daigneault together with the New York advertising agency Designframe. Six soft pastel shades and the basic elements of graphic design - lines, dots, squares, grid, grain and zigzag - give Elements its new exciting look. Tests have shown that the patterns incorporated in the paper are visible or disappear depending on the thickness and covering power of the printing inks used. If the sample is just visible, it supplements the print in such a way that interesting effects in the printing image can be attained without the coloured structure of the paper appearing overpowering or distracting. An interesting interaction between paper and print also develops. And, there is also a neutral version (solids).

Jim Sebastian from Designframe drew up a sample book which interprets the linguistic use of the design elements in funny graphics (e.g. square headed). Sebastian is very impressed by Strathmore and says of their relationship: "Working together with a paper manufacturer enables designers to advance art." To date, this cooperation was only limited to sales promotion. By jointly drawing up elements ranging from the conception to the market positioning, a truly new path is being taken. Horace Moses certainly would have approved.

## THE STRATHMORE GRADES

### Americana

Americana´s beautiful, pronounced surface, achieved by combining an authentic marking felt with a dandy roll pattern, is unique among text and cover papers. It is receptive to all printing and finishing techniques including four-color process, engraving, foil stamping, and dye cutting. It is particularly dramatic with embossing. Available in an array of acid-free whites, Americana comes in text and cover grades.

### Grandee

Richly textured Grandee offers exceptional choice, with four recycled, acid-free whites, a range of recycled colors, two virgin fiber colors, and four recycled duplex combinations. Grandee combines an authentic felt finish with a dandy roll pattern. Its outstanding opacity and ink holdout make it ideal for four-color process as well as all other printing and finishing techniques.

### Fiesta

Strathmore Fiesta is an acid-free, deckle-edged sheet now offered with the same authentic felt finish as Strathmore Pastelle. Its deckle edge is uniquely rendered in a choice of seven colors on white. By dressing up the envelope flap, the deckle is an excellent way to increase the overall impact of announcements and greeting cards. Fiesta is available in Text 80 (118g/qm) and in Cover 80 (216g/qm).

### Pastelle

With its subtle texture and deckle edge, Strathmore Pastelle offers a wide range of opportunities for creativity. Its fresh palette features three whites, one gray, and four soft colors. Authentic felt-finished, acid-free Pastelle is receptive to all printing and production techniques. Its high opacity, superior ink holdout, and deckle edge make it especially suited for social correspondence and high-end marketing communications.

### Rhododendron

A durable 25% cotton sheet with unique Telanian finish, Rhododendron offers the look and feel of handwoven Irish linen. It is available in three acid-free whites, three grays, black, and four sophisticated colors. Rhododendron´s 25% cotton content provides extra strength and durability for all applications. Its surface is exceptional for four-color process as well as for all other printing and production techniques.

### Renewal

Strathmore Renewal text and cover is a premium recycled paper containing 25% post-consumer and 25% pre-consumer recovered material by total fibre weight. The seven solid and seven fibre enhanced colors coordinate with each other in hue. The wove surface is ideal for all printing and production processes, from 4-color process, engraving and foil stamping to die cutting, embossing and scoring. Outstanding ink holdout and opacity make it ideal for all types of distinctive communication when quality and environmental concern are equally important.

### Writing System

This system offers a selection of fine correspondence papers from the Strathmore Writing System, America's most comprehensive and distinctive paper system for printed communications. Engineered to meet the needs of business into the next century, the Strathmore Writing system offers an unparalleled selection of virgin content and recycled, acid-free papers in coordinating finishes and colors. The writing weights of Strathmore Writing, Strathmore Pure Cotton, and Strathmore Script are backed by the Strathmore Laser Guarantee, ensuring their reliable performance in copy machines and laser printers.

### Elements

Strathmore Elements has an exceptionally smooth, level surface which guaranties excellent printability. The patterns are created with papermaking dyes applied by a unique manufacturing process. A solid version is also available. Six subtle colors were carefully designed to complement and coordinate with each other. The colors also coordinate with Strathmore Writing. This paper is an ideal choice for all printing and finishing techniques, from 4-color process, engraving and foil stamping to dye cutting, embossing, and scoring.

## STRATHMORE - WEIL PAPIER VIEL ZUM IMAGE BEITRÄGT

Die Zeiten des „Wilden Westens" waren in den Köpfen durchaus noch lebendig, als Horace Moses 1892 die Mittineague Paper Company in West Springfield, Massachusetts, gründete. Vielleicht benannte er seine Papierfabrik deshalb nach dem Indianerstamm, der in diesem Gebiet einmal gelebt hatte.

Moses´ Firmenphilosophie war ebenso einfach wie überzeugend: Er wollte außergewöhnliche, hochwertige Papiere produzieren und einen herausragenden Service bieten. Ständig suchte er nach neuen Papiermaschinen, mit denen er ausgefallene Sorten fertigen konnte. Er hatte davon gehört, daß es in England eine Maschine gab, die Büttenränder produzieren konnte, die handgeschöpftem Papier sehr ähnlich waren. Er reiste nach Europa, fand die Maschine und in Schottland auch gleich den Namen für seine Produkte: Strathmore.

Das landschaftlich wunderschöne Valley of Strathmore, in dem die Heide und die schottischen Disteln gerade in voller Blüte standen, hatte einen bleibenden Eindruck bei ihm hinterlassen. 1898 ließ er den Namen „Strathmore" als Warenzeichen eintragen und die Distel wurde zum Firmenlogo.

Horace Moses war davon überzeugt, daß er sehr gute Verkaufserfolge erzielen könnte, wenn er die Schönheit seiner Papiere in vielfältiger Weise zeigte. So ging er als Herausgeber des ersten Musterbuches mit Anwendungsbeispielen in die amerikanische Design-Geschichte ein. Er beschäftigte bei sich im Hause dafür eigens einen Drucker: Will Bradley erlangte später als Typographie-Designer und Drucker von hochwertigen Büchern Weltruhm.

Die Kunden nahmen die Musterbücher und so auch die Papiere mit Begeisterung auf, das Unternehmen expandierte. Unter den Neuerwerbungen befand sich auch eine Briefumschlagfabrik, die sicherstellte, daß es zu den einzelnen Papierqualitäten die passenden Umschläge in bekannter Strathmore Qualität gab.

Horace Moses starb 1947 im Alter von 85 Jahren, und die nachfolgenden Geschäftsführer erwiesen sich nicht immer als ebenso genial. 1962 wurde Strathmore an Hammermill verkauft und gehört seit 1986 zum größten Papierkonzern der Welt: Inter-national Paper.

### DIE PRODUKTPALETTE

Heute ist Strathmore ein führender Anbieter auf drei Spezialgebieten:

#### Baumwollhaltige Papiere

Bei den Sorten mit 25 % Baumwollanteil besitzt Strathmore in den USA den größten Anteil.

Dafür ist in erster Linie das Strathmore Writing System verantwortlich. Es wurde Ende der achtziger Jahre entwickelt und soeben vollständig überarbeitet und den Markterfordernissen angepaßt. Technische Verbesserungen machen einen problemlosen Einsatz auf allen Laserdruckern möglich. Die Farbpalette bietet außer verschiedenen Weißegraden auch „farbige Neutraltöne" an, die mit einem hohen Recyclinganteil hergestellt werden. Diese Farbtöne erwecken zwar den Eindruck eines farbigen Papieres, sind jedoch so flexibel einsetzbar wie ein weißes Papier.

#### Text und Cover Papiere

Bekannt ist Strathmore vor allem für seine farbigen Umschlagqualitäten. Authentische Filzmarkierungen sind das Markenzeichen dieser Papierfabrik. Die Qualitäten Grandee, Americana, Fiesta und Pastelle werden noch immer auf alten Papiermaschinen gefertigt, die beinahe im Handwerkertempo arbeiten. Viele Fabriken haben diese Technik bereits zugunsten wesentlich schnellerer Produktionsprozesse aufgegeben. Strathmore arbeitet hingegen ständig daran, diese Besonderheiten den Anforderungen des modernen Marktes anzupassen.

#### Künstlerpapiere

In den USA ist Strathmore Marktführer bei Künstlerpapieren. Die werden in einer Bandbreite von 100% Baumwollpapier bis hin zu komplett holzhaltigen Sorten angeboten. Als Bogenware oder als Zeichenblock kann man diese Papiere ausschließlich in den USA im Facheinzelhandel kaufen.

#### Ein modernes Marketingkonzept

Strathmore wendet sich in erster Linie an Grafikdesigner. Die haben einen entscheidenden Anteil bei der Papierauswahl und sind daran interessiert, stets neue Papierqualitäten und Anwendungsbeispiele zu erhalten. Der Trend entwickelt sich weg von reinen Papiermusterbüchern hin zu kombinierten Muster-und Anwendungsbüchern. Letztere zeigen Beispiele mit unterschiedlichen Drucktechniken, darunter auch Thermographie, Blindprägung, Folienkaschierung und Stahlstich. Damit lassen sich auf voluminösen Naturpapieren ungewöhnlich eindringliche Ergebnisse erzielen. Zu den Anwendungsbüchern gehören auch ausführliche technische Hinweise im Hinblick auf Litho, Druck und Weiterverarbeitung. Die Vorteile dieses Systems liegen auf der Hand:ein großer Fundus an Ideen ohne das Risiko des „Blindfluges" bei der Umsetzung in die Realität.

Der wird zudem durch eine sachkundige Beratung vermieden. Seit 1958 schult Strathmore in Amerika die „Graphic Art Consultants" der Vertriebspartner - das sind Papiergroßhändler in 35 Ländern der Erde. Das mehrtägige Seminar unterrichtet die Agenturberater über die Rolle des Papieres im Grafikdesign, verschiedene Drucktechniken sowie neueste Trends in Sachen Papier und Design. Von den speziell eingesetzten Beratern erhalten Werbeagenturen oft die Anregungen und Informationen, die der Drucker mangels Zeit oder Kenntnissen nicht geben kann.

In der Angebotsbreite hat sich Strathmore auf den Bedarf der Werbeagenturen eingestellt. Von jeder Sorte wird ein Komplettprogramm angeboten, d.h. mehrere Gewichte im Papier- und Kartonbereich sowie Briefhüllen und passende Etiketten.

Strathmore hat eine europäische Zentrale in Bussum, Niederlande. Von dort erhalten die europäischen Großhändler eine speziell auf ihren Markt abgestimmte Verkaufsunterstützung. Das eigene Lagerhaus ermöglicht eine Belieferung innerhalb weniger Tage.

**Die neueste Entwicklung**

Umfangreiche Marktforschungen haben gezeigt, wie der Papierbedarf in der zweiten Hälfte der neunziger Jahre voraussichtlich aussehen wird.

Zentrale Forderung ist die Umweltverträglichkeit. Aus diesem Grund werden bei Strathmore nur noch Papiere produziert, die je nach Qualitätsanforderungen einen größtmöglichen Recyclinganteil besitzen. Auch der Einsatz von Baumwolle ist ökologisch sinnvoll, da es sich um einen vergleichsweise schnell nachwachsenden Rohstoff handelt. In der Papierproduktion werden zudem nur die zur Textilherstellung nicht geeigneten Randschichten der Baumwolle eingesetzt.

Ein weiterer Trend: Papier muß den Anforderungen an moderne Bürodrucker und neueste Schnelldruckmaschinen gerecht werden. Dazu brauchen sie eine relativ glatte und geschlossene Oberfläche, einen speziellen Feuchtegehalt und sollten auch im A 4 Format angeboten werden. Last but not least fordern die Werbetreibenden, daß auch ein hochwertiges Papier bezahlbar sein muß. Das Ergebnis dieser Erkenntnisse hat bei Strathmore einen Namen: Elements. Eine umweltverträgliche Stoffzusammensetzung (60% Recyclinganteil) , die von der Fabrik garantierte Eignung für den Laserdrucker (bis 105 g/qm) und kostet ungefähr 10 % weniger als vergleichbare Sorten.

Das Papier entwickelte Produktmanager Bob Daigneault zusammen mit der New Yorker Werbeagentur Designframe. Sechs zarte Pastelltöne und die Grundelemente grafischer Gestaltung - lines, dots, squares, grid, grain und zickzack - geben Elements die neue ungewöhnliche Optik. Versuche zeigen, daß die im Papier eingebrachten Muster je nach Farbdichte und Deckfähigkeit der verwendeten Druckfarben sichtbar sind oder verschwinden. Ist das Muster gerade noch sichtbar, ergänzt es den Druck so, daß interessante Effekte im Druckbild entstehen können, ohne daß die farbige Struktur des Papieres dabei aufdringlich oder störend wirkt. Es kann sich eine ebenso interessante wie witzige Beziehung zwischen Papier und Druck entwickeln. Es gibt aber auch eine neutrale Version (solids).

Jim Sebastian von Designframe entwarf ein Musterbuch, das die sprachliche Verwendung der Gestaltungselemente in witzige Grafiken umsetzt (z.B. square-headed ). Sebastian ist sehr angetan von der Zusammenarbeit mit Strathmore: „Mit einem Papierhersteller zusammenzuarbeiten, ermöglicht es Designern, die Kunst voranzutreiben." Bisher war diese Zusammenarbeit nur auf die Absatzförderung beschränkt. Die gemeinsame Erarbeitung von Elements von der Konzeption bis hin zur Positionierung im Markt stellt ein echtes Novum dar. Daran hätte Horace Moses sicher seine Freude gehabt.

**STRATHMORE -DIE PAPIERQUALITÄTEN**

Americana hat eine sehr grobe, wellenartige Filznarbung. Je nach Betrachtungshaltung wird eine andere Oberflächenstruktur sichtbar- ein Papier mit multidimensionalen Effekten. Americana hat einen Recyclinganteil von 50%, ist in 11 kräftigen Farben und zwei Gewichten erhältlich; es wird vor allem als Umschlagqualität eingesetzt.

**Grandee**

ist die bekannteste filzgenarbte Sorte. Die strukturierte Oberfläche wird mit dem Egoutteur und im Anschluß an die Siebpartie mit Trockenfilzen erzielt. Grandee hat einen Altpapieranteil von 50% , ist in 13 Farben und zwei Gewichten erhältlich; durch die gute Farbwiedergabe und die hohe Opazität ist es ein geeigneter Druckträger für alle Arten von Druckobjekten.

**Fiest**

hat etwas wirklich Ungewöhnliches zu bieten, nämlich einen farbigen Büttenrand an den beiden langen Seiten. 9 Farbvarianten in zwei Gewichten machen dieses Papier zum idealen Trägermaterial für ausgefallene Einladungskarten, Glückwunschkarten oder Speisekarten.

**Pastelle**

hat eine authentische Filznarbung und einen Büttenrand an den beiden langen Seiten. Durch die elegante Farbpalette mit 12 feinabgestimmten Pastelltönen ist Pastelle das richtige Papier für alle Kommunikation im Bereich hochwertiger Markenartikel.

**Rhododendron**

ist die einzige geprägte Sorte im Programm. Das Muster, das handgewebtem irischem Leinen nachempfunden wurde, gibt diesem Papier mit 25% Baumwollanteil die elegant sportliche Note. Die Angebotsbreite von 2 Gewichten und 14 Farben macht es möglich, Rhododendron überall da einzusetzen, wo man die Verbindung von traditionellen Werten mit modernem Design demonstrieren möchte.

**Renewal**

hat eine maschinenglatte Oberfläche. Das Besondere an diesem umweltfreundlichen Papier mit 50% Recyclinganteil ist der Fasereinschluß. Zu den 7 Farben in der Version „dirty" gibt es auch noch die Variante „clean": das sind die gleichen Farben, aber ohne Fasereinschlüsse. Renewal dokumentiert auf ästhetisch ansprechende Weise Umweltbewußtsein.

**Writing System**

ist ein umfassendes Programm verschiedener Papiere für den Geschäftspostbereich. Man kann wählen zwischen 12 zarten Farbtönen, verschiedenen Oberflächen und unterschiedlicher Stoffzusammensetzung. Dazu gibt es passende Etiketten und Briefhüllen. Ebenso hat man die Wahl zwischen Ausführungen mit und ohne Wasserzeichen. Dem Einsatzzweck entsprechend ist das Papier garantiert im Laserdrucker zu bedrucken und für Inkjet geeignet.

**Elements**

Elements ist farblich auf Strathmore Writing abgestimmt und in das Strathmore Writing System integriert.

Das Papier ist aufgrund seine technischen Eigenschaften universell einsetzbar, d.h. sowohl als Geschäftsausstattungspapier (Laserdruckgarantie) als auch als Auflagen- und Umschlagqualität.

## STRATHMORE - PARCE QUE LE PAPIER C'EST PARTIE DE L'IMAGE DE MARQUE

L'ère du Far West était encore bien vivante dans les esprits lorsque Horace Moses fonda en 1892 la Mittineague Paper Company à West Springfield, Massachussetts. C'est peut-être pour cette raison qu'il a donné à sa fabrique de papier le nom d'une tribu indienne qui avait vécu dans la région.

La philosophie d'entreprise de Moses était aussi simple que convaincante. Il voulait produire des papiers de qualité supérieure, sortant de l'ordinaire, et proposer des services exceptionnels. Il était sans cesse à la recherche de nouvelles machines à papier qui lui permettent de fabriquer des types de papier peu communs. Il avait entendu dire qu'il existait en Angleterre une machine avec laquelle il était possible d'obtenir des bords frangeux ressemblant à s'y tromper à du papier à la cuve. Il se rendit donc en Europe, y trouva la machine qu'il cherchait et trouva par la même occasion un nom pour ses produits en Ecosse: Strathmore.

Le paysage pittoresque de la „Valley of Strathmore", où la bruyère et les chardons écossais étaient justement en fleurs, lui avait laissé un souvenir inoubliable. En 1898, il fit enregistrer le nom de „Strathmore" comme marque déposée et le chardon devint l'emblème de sa firme.

Horace Moses était persuadé que ses papiers auraient beaucoup de succès à la vente s'il parvenait à montrer leur beauté sous les formes les plus diverses. C'est ainsi qu'il est entré dans l'histoire du design américain en tant qu'éditeur du premier catalogue d'échantillons avec exemples d'applications. Il avait engagé spécialement dans ce but un imprimeur dans sa firme: Will Bradley allait se faire par la suite une réputation mondiale en tant que designer typographique et imprimeur de livres de haute valeur.

Les clients firent un accueil enthousiaste au catalogue d'échantillons ainsi qu'aux papiers et l'entreprise prit de l'extension. Une de ses nouvelles acquisitions, une fabrique d'enveloppes, allait lui permettre de proposer des enveloppes allant avec les différents types de papier, tout en restant fidèle à la légendaire qualité Strathmore.

Horace Moses décéda en 1947 à l'âge de 85 ans, et les gérants qui prirent sa succession n'étaient pas tous aussi géniaux que lui. En 1962, Strathmore fut vendu à Hammermill; depuis 1986, elle fait partie du plus grand groupe de fabrication de papier du monde: International Paper.

### LA GAMME DE PRODUITS

Strathmore est de nos jours un des plus grands fournisseurs de papier dans trois domaines spécialisés:

#### Papiers à base de coton

C'est Strathmore qui détient aux USA la part la plus importante des types de papier renfermant 25 % de coton. Le mérite en revient avant tout au Strathmore Writing System. Ce système a été mis au point à la fin des années quatre-vingt et vient d'être entièrement remanié et adapté aux besoins du marché. Grâce aux perfectionnements techniques qui lui ont été apportés, il peut être utilisé sans problèmes sur toutes les imprimantes laser. A côté de différentes qualités de blanc, la gamme de coloris comporte également des „tons neutres de couleur" dans la fabrication desquels les pâtes de recyclage représentent un pourcentage élevé. Tout en étant de couleur, les papiers fabriqués dans ces coloris sont néanmoins utilisables avec autant de souplesse qu'un papier blanc.

#### Papiers „Text & Cover"

Strathmore est connue avant tout pour ses qualités de carton de couleur. Leurs marques de feutre authen-tiques sont l'emblème de cette fabrique de papier. Les qualités Grandee, Americana, Fiesta et Pastelle sont encore fabriquées de nos jours sur les machines à papier d'antan, qui ne travaillent guère plus vite qu'un artisan. Bien des fabriques ont déjà abandonné cette technique pour se tourner vers des processus de production beaucoup plus rapides. Strathmore au contraire s'efforce continuellement de concilier ces particularités avec les exigences du marché moderne.

#### Papier de dessin et peinture

Aux USA, Strathmore est le numéro un sur le marché des papiers de dessin et peinture. Ceux-ci vont des papiers 100 % coton aux pâtes entièrement à base de bois. Ces papiers sont en vente exclusive aux USA dans le commerce de détail spécialisé, par feuilles ou en blocs.

#### Un concept moderne de marketing

Strathmore s'adresse avant tout aux dessinateurs graphistes. Car ceux-ci jouent un rôle décisif dans le choix du papier; de plus, ils sont toujours à la recherche de nouvelles qualités de papier et de nouveaux exemples d'applications. La tendance est non plus au simple catalogue d'échantillons, mais au catalogue combiné d'échantillons et d'applications. Des exemples des différentes techniques d'impression, entre autres thermographie, gaufrage à froid, contrecollage et gravure sur acier, y sont présentés. Cela permet d'obtenir des résultats du plus bel effet sur les papiers non couchés volumineux. Les catalogues d'applications renferment également des renseignements techniques détaillés sur la lithographie, l'impression et la transformation des papiers. Les avantages de ce système sont clairs: Il offre une mine d'idées qui peuvent être mises en oeuvre dans la pratique sans devoir se lancer à l'aveuglette. Un service compétent d'information contribue par ailleurs à éliminer les risques. Strathmore propose depuis 1958 des stages de formation en Amérique aux „graphic art consultants" de ses partenaires de distribution - des grossistes en papier de 35 pays du monde. Ce séminaire, qui dure plusieurs jours, informe les consultants des agences de publicité sur le rôle du papier dans le design graphique, sur les différentes techniques d'impression ainsi que sur les tendances nouvelles en matière de papier et de design. Et ce sont bien souvent les consultants qui fournissent aux agences de publicité les idées et les informations que l'imprimeur n'est pas en mesure de leur donner faute de temps ou de connaissances.

Strathmore a adapté son offre aux besoins des agences de publicité. La firme propose un programme complet pour chaque type de papier, c.-à-d. plusieurs grammages de papier et de carton ainsi que les enveloppes et les étiquettes correspondantes.

Strathmore a un siège central en Europe, à Bussum, Pays-

Bas. Celui-ci apporte aux grossistes européens un soutien spécialement adapté à leurs marchés respectifs. Son entrepôt lui permet d'effectuer des livraisons en quelques jours seulement.

**La toute dernière évolution**

Des études de marché détaillées ont montré quels seront vraisemblablement les besoins en papier durant la deuxième moitié des années 90. Une des exigences premières sera l'absence de pollution pour l'environnement. Pour cette raison, Strathmore ne fabrique plus que des papiers utilisant le pourcentage maximum de pâte de recyclage possible en fonction des exigences de qualité. L'utilisation du coton est également favorable sur le plan écologique car il s'agit d'une matière première renouvelable rapidement comparée aux autres matières. De plus, seules les couches marginales du coton, qui ne sont pas utilisées dans la fabrication textile, entrent dans la fabrication du papier.

Autre tendance: Le papier doit répondre aux exigences imparties aux imprimantes modernes de bureau et aux derniers modèles de machines à imprimer rapides. Il doit donc avoir une surface relativement lisse et fermée et doit également être proposé en format A4. Last but not least, les publicitaires attendent des papiers de qualité supérieure qu'ils soient néanmoins de prix abordable.

La somme de toutes ces exigences a un nom chez Strathmore: Elements. Ses caractéristiques: composition non polluante du papier (part des pâtes de recyclage 60 %), compatibilité garantie avec les imprimantes laser (jusqu'à 105 g/m2), coût approximatif: 10 % de moins que les types de papier comparables.

Ce papier a été mis au point par le chef de produit Bob Daigneault en collaboration avec l'agence de publicité new-yorkaise Designframe. Six tons pastel très doux et les éléments du design graphique - lines, dots, squares, grid, grain et zigzag - confèrent à Elements son aspect peu ordinaire. Des tests ont montré que les dessins dans le papier sont plus ou moins visibles, jusqu'à devenir invisibles, selon la densité spectrale et le pouvoir couvrant des encres d'imprimerie utilisées. Si le motif est à peine visible, il permet d'obtenir, combiné avec l'impression, des effets intéressants sans que la structure de couleur du papier soit trop voyante ou gênante. Il en résulte une interaction à la fois intéressante et amusante entre le papier et l'impression. Mais il existe également une version neutre (solids).

Jim Sebastian de l'agence Designframe a créé un catalogue d'échantillons où les éléments d'un nom sont remplacés par des symboles graphiques combinés de manière amusante (p. ex. square-headed). Sebastian est très satisfait de la collaboration avec Strathmore: „Travailler avec un fabricant de papier permet aux designers de faire progresser l'art.“ Jusqu'ici, cette collaboration était limitée à la promotion des ventes. L'élaboration en commun d'Elements, de la conception au positionnement sur le marché, est une nouveauté sans précédent. Et cela aurait certainement fait très plaisir à Horace Moses.

Les papiers Strathmore sont en vente chez (revendeur du pays concerné). Il faut s'attendre à des délais de livraison longs pour les types de papier non disponibles de stock.

**STRATHMORE - LES QUALITÉS DE PAPIER**

**Americana**

porte une marque de feutre ondulée très accentuée. Sa structure de surface varie selon l'angle du regard - un papier aux effets multidimensionnels. Americana comporte 50 % de matière recyclée ; il est disponible en 11 coloris soutenus et deux poids - il est tout particulièrement employé pour les couvertures.

**Grandee**

est le plus renommé parmi les papiers marqués au feutre. Sa surface structurée est obtenue par le passage sur l'égoutteur puis sur la table de fabrication à feutres sécheurs. Grandee est composé à 50 % de vieux papiers recyclés : il est disponible en 13 coloris et deux poids - grâce à une bonne reproduction des couleurs et à une opacité élevée, il forme un excellent support d'impression.

**Fiesta**

est un papier peu ordinaire qui se distingue par des bords frangeux colorés qui longent la feuille.

9 coloris et deux poids font de ce papier un support idéal pour des cartes d'invitation, des cartes de vœux ou des menus originaux.

**Pastelle**

présente une marque de feutre authentique ainsi que des bords frangeux le long de la feuille.

Avec sa gamme de coloris élégants comportant 12 nuances pastel harmonieuses, Pastelle est parfaitement adapté à tout ce qui touche à la communication dans le secteur des articles de marque.

**Rhododendron**

est le seul papier gaufré de la gamme. Son motif inspiré du lin irlandais tissé à la main procure une touche d'élégance sportive à ce papier qui contient 25 % de coton.

2 poids et 14 coloris permettent d'utiliser Rhododendron à chaque fois que l'on souhaite combiner les valeurs traditionnelles et le design moderne.

**Renewal**

possède une surface satinée sur calandre. Respectueux de l'environnement avec 50 % de matière recyclée, ce papier se distingue par des insertions de fibres. Il est disponible en 7 coloris, avec insertions pour la version „dirty" et sans insertions pour la version „clean."

Renewal est l'expression réussie d'une alliance entre l'esthétique et le respect de l'environnement.

**Writing System**

est une gamme complète de différents papiers destinés à la correspondance commerciale. On a le choix entre 12 couleurs tendres, différentes surfaces et combinaisons de chiffons. Viennent s'y ajouter étiquettes et enveloppes assorties. Il y a également possibilité d'opter ou non pour une marque filigranée. Comme l'exige son domaine d'utilisation, il est adapté aux imprimantes laser ou à jet d'encre.

**Elements**

Les coloris de Elements s'harmonisent avec Strathmore Writing et s'intègrent au

**Strathmore Writing System.**

Grâce à ses qualités techniques, ce papier est utilisable dans tous les domaines, c'est-à-dire aussi bien au bureau (impression laser garantie), que pour l'édition de brochures ou la fabrication de couvertures.

## STRATHMORE PAPERS AND BECKETT PAPERS OFFICES AND MERCHANTS WORLDWIDE

**STRATHMORE PAPERS**
Two Gateway Boulevard
East Granby, CT 06026 (USA)
phone: (+1) 860 844 2525
fax: (+1) 860 844 2550

Strathmore Papers is part of INTERNATIONAL PAPER'S Fine Papers Division
To receive more information about Strathmore Papers and your home merchant, please contact one of the following offices.

UNITED STATES:
Strathmore Papers is represented in every state of the union.
For full information please contact (+1) 800 423 7313 or the Fine Paper Head Office East Granby, CT 06026 USA
Margaret E. Conklin,
phone: (+1) 860 844 2404
fax: (+1) 860 844 2551

EUROPE, MIDDLE EAST, AND AFRICA:
Strathmore Beckett International
Oude Apeldoornseweg 26
7333 NS Apeldoom,
The Netherlands
Gitte Demmers
phone (+31) 55 5384553
fax: (+31) 55 5384550
Strathmore is represented in the following countries:
Austria: IT Papier, Belgium: PB Papier NV, Cyprus: George G. Kazinos & Co., Denmark: Albatross Papir, France: Aussedat Rey Distribution, Germany: Schneidersöhne Papier, Israel: Prelude Ltd, Italy: Perego Carta, Malta: Beck Graphis Ltd, Norway: Carl Emil AS, Portugal: Spectra, Spain: Royal Paper & Co., Switzerland: Mühleback AG Graphic, Sweden: Svenskt Papper AB, The Netherlands: Lutkie & Smit Papier and Scaldia Papier, Turkey: Unirep Trading & Agency Inc., United Kingdom: G.F. Smith & Son Ltd. Kenya: Proost Paper Ltd. , South Africa: Spicers

CARIBBEAN, CENTRAL-AND SOUTH AMERICA
Sales Office in Memphis, TN 38197 USA
Julio Cepeda,
phone: (+1) 901 763 7613
fax: (+1) 901 763 7169
Strathmore is represented in the following countries:
Argentina: Dimagraf SACI, Bolivia: GMS Bolivia, Brazil: VIP Papers, Chile: GMS Productos Graficos, Colombia: Bico Inter-national, Guatemala: Codelsa, Jamaica: H.G.M. Walker Ltd., Mexico: Importaciones y Distribuciones Lumen SA de CV., Peru: GMS Distribuidora Grafica S.A., Puerto Rico: American Paper Corporation, Uruguay: José Castiglioni S.A., Venezuela: Casa Hellmund & CIA S.A.

ASIA AND THE PACIFIC:
Sales Office in Hong Kong
Albert C. Lau,
phone: (+852) 2586 8818
fax: (+852) 2824 3035
Strathmore is represented in the following countries:
China: Hiap Moh Paper, Indonesia: PT Armada Pratama and PT Surya Palacejaya, Japan: JMC Corporation, Malaysia: Hiap Moh Paper Co. (m) Sdn. Bhd., Phillippines: Star Paper Corporation, Singapore: Hiap Moh Corporation, Taiwan R.O.C.: Circle Trading Company Ltd., Thailand: D.H.A.Siamwalle Ltd. Australia: Alexander Moir & Co. Pty. Ltd., K.W. Dogelt Pty. Ltd., Bommerang Paper, New Zealand: B.J. Ball Papers

**BECKETT PAPERS**
Two Gateway Boulevard
East Granby, CT 06026 USA
phone: (+1) 800 543 1188
fax: (+1) 800 392 9192

Beckett Papers is part of INTERNATIONAL PAPER'S Fine Papers Division
To recieve more information about Beckett Papers and your home merchant, please contact one of the following offices:

UNITED STATES:
Beckett Papers is represented in every state of the union.
For full information please contact (+1) 800 423 2259 or the Fine Paper Head Office East Granby, CT 06026
Jeannie Means,
phone: (+1) 860 844 2413
fax: (+1) 860 844 2552

EUROPE, MIDDLE EAST, AND AFRICA
Strathmore Beckett International
Oude Apeldoornseweg 26
7333 NS Apeldoom,
The Netherlands
Gitte Demmers
phone (+31) 55 5384553
fax: (+31) 55 5384550
Beckett is represented in the following countries:
Austria: Europapier and Eu-RO Handelsgellschaft m.b.H., Belgium: Epacar, Cyprus: George G. Kazinos & Co., Denmark: Albatross Papir, France: Muller Renage, Germany: Römerturm, Israel: Prelude Ltd, Italy: Perego Carta, Norway: Carl Emil AS, Portugal: Spectra, Spain: Papelera del Gaya, Switzerland: Mühlebach AG Graphic, Sweden: Svenskt Papper AB, The Netherlands: Bührmann-Ubbens Papier, United Kingdom: G.F. Smith & Son, Ltd., Kenya: Proost Paper (E.A.) Ltd. South Africa: Spicers

CARIBBEAN, CENTRAL- AND SOUTH AMERICA
Sales Office in Memphis, TN, 38197, USA
Julio Cepeda,
phone: (+1) 901 763 7613
fax: (+1) 901 763 7169
Beckett is represented in the following countries:
Argentina: Dimagraf SACI, Bolivia: GMS Bolivia, Brazil: VIP Papers, Chile: GMS Productos Graficos, Colombia: Propal SA, Guatemala: Codelsa, Honduras: AM Capens & Sons Inc., Jamaica: H.G.M. Walker Ltd., Mexico: Importaciones y Distribuciones Lumen SA de CV., Peru: GMS Distribuidora Grafica S.A., Puerto Rico: American Paper Corporation, Uruguay: José Castiglioni S.A., Venezuela: Dasa Hellmund +CIA S.A.

ASIA AND THE PACIFIC:
Sales office in Hong Kong
Albert C. Lau,
phone: (+852) 2586 8818,
fax: (+852) 2824 3035
Beckett is represented in the following countries:
China: Hiap Moh Paper, Indonesia: PT Armada Pratama and PT Surya Palacejaya, Japan: JMC Corporation, Korea: Kye Sung Corporation and Yousun Corporation, Malaysia: Hiap Moh Paper Co. (M) Sdn. Bhd., Phillippines: Star Paper Corporation, Singapore: Hiap Moh Corporation, Taiwan R.O.C.: Circle Trading Company Ltd., Thailand: D.H.A. Siamwalle Ltd. Australia: Alexander Moir & Co. Pty. Ltd., K.W. Dogelt Pty. Ltd., Boomerang Paper, New Zealand: B.J. Ball Papers